SpringerBriefs in Economics

More information about this series at http://www.springer.com/series/8876

Dan S. Felsenthal · Hannu Nurmi

Voting Procedures for Electing a Single Candidate

Proving Their (In)Vulnerability to Various Voting Paradoxes

Springer

Dan S. Felsenthal
School of Political Sciences
University of Haifa
Haifa
Israel

Hannu Nurmi
Department of Political Science
University of Turku
Turku
Finland

ISSN 2191-5504 ISSN 2191-5512 (electronic)
SpringerBriefs in Economics
ISBN 978-3-319-74032-4 ISBN 978-3-319-74033-1 (eBook)
https://doi.org/10.1007/978-3-319-74033-1

Library of Congress Control Number: 2017963840

Printed on acid-free paper

This Springer imprint is published by the registered company Springer International Publishing AG part of Springer Nature
The registered company address is: Gewerbestrasse 11, 6330 Cham, Switzerland

Preface

Free and fair elections are an essential ingredient of democratic governance. Elections without these attributes can be and have been held, but their connection with 'the government of the people, by the people and for the people', as Abraham Lincoln succinctly put it, is tenuous at best. This book focuses on the fairness part of the elections. More specifically, we aim to evaluate voting procedures—those in everyday use and those invented but not yet employed—from the point of view of how faithfully they reflect the opinions of the voters. It turns out that teasing out the will of the people from the opinions expressed in voting ballots is not at all straightforward. On the contrary, several mutually exclusive intuitions about what constitutes being the collectively best candidate, or collectively most desirable policy alternative, can be found in the scholarly literature and in political parlance. Indeed, the social choice theory is known for its results establishing incompatibilities of various desiderata that one could expect the choice rules—and voting procedures among them—to satisfy.

This book is a summary of some of the work that has been done on voting procedures over the past decades by numerous authors including us. Its core text is the first-named author's extensive article (Felsenthal 2012), and this book is an updated and extended version of that text. Many findings reported here are, however, based on our earlier work in this area (e.g. Felsenthal & Tideman 2013, 2014; Felsenthal & Nurmi 2016, 2017; Nurmi 1983, 1987, 1999, 2012) and some are published here for the first time.

Although the list of properties or desiderata of voting procedures that we deal with is rather long, it is by no means exhaustive. We have focused on properties that have acquired most attention in the scholarly debates. We are particularly interested in various articulations of the notion of winning of elections and in examining the very rationale of voting. This book can be considered as a companion text of our *Monotonicity Failures Afflicting Procedures for Electing a Single Candidate* (Felsenthal & Nurmi 2017) where the properties related to the rationale of participation are in the primary focus. That book along with the present one gives—we hope—a reasonably broad basis for evaluating voting procedures and—when augmented with situational parameters—making enlightened choices among them.

However, the study of the main paradoxes afflicting various voting procedures cannot be complete before the necessary and/or sufficient conditions under which a given paradox can occur under a given voting procedure are known. As most such conditions are still unknown, the relative desirability of the various voting procedures must continue to be assessed without robust knowledge regarding the probability of their occurrence.

Nevertheless, in assessing the relative desirability of various voting procedures, we hope that this book will be useful not only to social choice theorists and students but also to students and researchers in related areas concerned with aspects of decision-making by vote: political science, mathematics, economics, business administration and constitutional law. It can also be used as a textbook in social choice courses and, therefore, we included several exercises (and answers to these exercises) at the end of each chapter of this book.

In the course of decades when studying voting procedures individually and jointly, we have incurred numerous intellectual debts, indeed, too numerous for all of them to be explicitly mentioned here. So we just want to extend our thanks to our former co-authors in this field: Paul R. Abramson, Fuad Aleskerov, Adiel Teixeira de Almeida, Sven Berg, Steven J. Brams, Avraham Brichta, Vincent Chua, Abraham Diskin, Mario Fedrizzi, Manfred J. Holler, Janusz Kacprzyk, Moshé Machover, Ze'ev Maoz, Tommi Meskanen, Nicholas Miller, Per Molander, Lasse Nurmi, Amnon Rapoport, Donald G. Saari, Nicolaus Tideman and Slawomir Zadrozny.

We are also grateful to Dr. Martina Bihn—the Editorial Director Business/Economics & Statistics at Springer—for her excellent and smooth cooperation; and to Judith Kripp and Kay Stoll of Springer's staff, as well as to Sooryadeepth Jayakrishnan of Scientific Publishing Services Ltd., India, who made the publication of this book in its present form possible.

Jerusalem, Israel — Dan S. Felsenthal
Turku, Finland — Hannu Nurmi

References

Felsenthal, D. S. (2012). Review of paradoxes afflicting procedures for electing a single candidate. In D. S. Felsenthal & M. Machover (Eds.), *Electoral systems: Paradoxes, assumptions, and procedures* (pp. 19–92). Berlin, Heidelberg: Springer, Chap. 3.

Felsenthal, D. S., & Nurmi, H. (2016). Two types of participation failure under nine voting methods in variable electorates. *Public Choice, 168*, 115–135.

Felsenthal, D. S., & Nurmi, H. (2017). *Monotonicity failures afflicting procedures for electing a single candidate.* Cham, Switzerland: Springer.

Felsenthal, D. S., & Tideman, N. (2013). Varieties of failure of monotonicity and participation under five voting methods. *Theory and Decision, 75*, 59–77.

Felsenthal, D. S. & Tideman, N. (2014). Interacting double monotonicity failure with direction of impact under five voting methods. *Mathematical Social Sciences, 67*, 57–66.

Nurmi, H. (1983). Voting procedures: A summary analysis. *British Journal of Political Science, 13*, 181–208.

Nurmi, H. (1987). *Comparing voting systems.* Dordrect: D. Reidel.

Nurmi, H. (1999). *Voting paradoxes and how to deal with them.* Berlin, Heidelberg, New York: Springer

Nurmi, H. (2012). On the relevance of theoretical results to voting system choice. In D. S. Felsenthal & M. Machover (Eds.), *Electoral systems: paradoxes, assumptions, and procedures* (pp. 255–274). Berlin, Heidelberg: Springer, Chap.10.

Contents

Chapter 1
Introduction

Abstract Voting is a common way to resolve disagreements regarding policies to be adopted or candidates to be chosen for various positions and is therefore a necessary ingredient of democratic government. Yet there are numerous voting rules that differ from each other in processing the ballots into voting results. In other words, it is possible that for a given set of voters having a fixed distribution of preferences among the competing alternatives, one would obtain the election of a different alternative as a result of using a different voting rule. We focus on the most obvious desiderata associated with voting procedures, viz., the avoidance of paradoxical outcomes.

Keywords Voting procedures · Berlin versus Bonn vote · Procedure–dependence of voting outcomes · Voting system desiderata

Voting is a common way to resolve disagreements regarding policies to be adopted or candidates to be chosen for various positions. Sometimes the actual balloting is preceded by a lengthy process of negotiation whereby various alternatives are being introduced, defended, opposed and evaluated. Once it is found that no unanimity about the policy or candidate to be chosen prevails in the community, voting is resorted to as the final arbiter of the disagreement. Sometimes the decision to take the vote is constitutionally or otherwise predetermined and no specific decision to resort to voting is needed. Even so, voting is, indeed, a very common way to make collective decisions. In the light of this, it is surprising to find that there are many different procedures that are used to achieve apparently the same goal, viz., to single out the collectively best alternative or candidate, "the will of the people", as it is sometimes called.

In his *magnum opus* Riker (1982) demonstrated that in general it is not the case that the outcome of the voting—no matter which procedure is in use—would unquestionably be the "correct one". Indeed, Riker tries to convince us that the notion of the will of the people lacks an unambiguous meaning. The reasons are three–fold:

D. S. Felsenthal and H. Nurmi, *Voting Procedures for Electing a Single Candidate*, SpringerBriefs in Economics, https://doi.org/10.1007/978-3-319-74033-1_1

First, all voting procedures are vulnerable to strategic misrepresentation of opinions in the sense that at least theoretically situations emerge where it is in the voters' interest not to vote according to their true preferences. So, says Riker, the outside observer or ballot return official can never be sure that the ballots submitted reflect the true opinions of the voters. Therefore, no matter how accurately the voters' ballots are aggregated into collective choices, there is no assurance that what has been aggregated is, in fact, the opinions of the people.

Second, when one must select one out of three or more alternatives the will of the majority of the people may turn out to be cyclical (intransitive): a majority of the people may prefer alternative A to B, a majority (composed of different people) may prefer alternative B to C, and a majority (composed of another set of voters) may prefer alternative C to A. In this case—which is known in the literature as *the Paradox of Voting*—the will of the majority of the people is unclear and the act of voting may be considered as meaningless.

Third, voting procedures aim at decisiveness no matter how the opinions are distributed among voters and yet there are opinion distributions (voting situations) where seemingly plausible voting systems result in different winners. Riker discusses several such situations, but let us illustrate this with the following purely fictitious example involving the election of the US president from the following set of candidates: Bloomberg, Bush, Clinton, Sanders, Trump. Let us assume the following distribution (profile) of opinions among 90 million voters (cf. Table 1.1 below).

The table indicates that 40 million voters order the candidates so that Trump is their favorite, followed by Bush, thereafter Sanders, then Bloomberg and finally Clinton, or slightly more formally, $Trump \succ Bush \succ Sanders \succ Bloomberg \succ Clinton$. The other opinions are indicated in the same manner. Now, suppose that only the opinions have been given, but the voting procedure is yet to be determined. Suppose, furthermore, that the one–person one–vote, or Plurality Voting, is being used. Then it is reasonable to assume that Trump gets 40 million, Clinton 30 million and Bloomberg 20 million votes, whereupon Trump wins.

Suppose that the constitution requires that whoever wins has to be supported by more than 50% of the electorate and that if this requirement is not satisfied by any candidate in terms of the one–person one–vote principle, there will be a second round of voting where only the two candidates with the largest number of votes can participate. Since the two largest vote–getters on the first count are Trump and Clinton, neither of whom gets more than 45 million votes, the 20 million voters whose favorite is Bloomberg now determine the winner (since we can assume that the Clinton and Trump supporters will vote for their favorite also on the second

Table 1.1 A fictitious preference profile over five candidates

40 million	30 million	20 million
Trump	Clinton	Bloomberg
Bush	Bloomberg	Sanders
Sanders	Bush	Bush
Bloomberg	Sanders	Clinton
Clinton	Trump	Trump

round). They prefer Clinton to Trump. Hence the former gets 50 million votes on the second round and emerges as the winner.

Looking at Table 1.1 from the angle of pairwise comparison of candidates, we could conduct all 10 (5 × 4/2) comparisons involving different pairs of candidates and tally the number of victories of each candidate assuming that the winner of each comparison is the candidate that receives more votes than its contestant. The tally reveals that there is a candidate that defeats by a majority of votes every other candidate in such comparisons. This candidate is Bloomberg. All others suffer at least one defeat in those comparisons. In the theory of voting a candidate that defeats all others in pairwise comparisons is called the *Condorcet Winner*. As will be seen in the following there are several voting procedures that end up with a Condorcet Winner whenever there is one in the voting profile. These procedures are called *Condorcet extensions* or *Condorcet–consistent* procedures. In the example of Table 1.1 all Condorcet extension voting procedures elect Bloomberg.

Suppose that each candidate is given a number of points by each voter in accordance with the rank that the candidate occupies in the voter's preferences so that the last (lowest) ranked candidate receives 0 points, the penultimate candidate 1 point, the third lowest 2 points, and so on. Suppose, moreover, that the procedure elects the candidate with the largest sum of points given by each voter. In Table 1.1 this procedure, which is known as the Borda count, would yield Bush the winner (with 220 million points).

All candidates except Sanders have now been rendered winners by varying the procedure, while keeping the voter opinions fixed. With an additional *ad hoc* assumption we can make also Sanders the winner by using the Approval Voting procedure whereby each voter may vote for as many candidates as he/she wishes with the restriction that each candidate can be given either 0 or 1 vote. Making the *ad hoc* assumption that all voters in the left–most voter group of 40 million vote for their three highest ranked candidates, while all the other voters vote for their two highest ranked candidates, Sanders emerges as the Approval Voting winner in this example (with 60 million votes).

So, each candidate may become the winner in this fictitious profile. Admittedly this is a highly special profile and no suggestion is here made regarding its likelihood in practice. The point of the example, however, is to illustrate the oft–cited claim that voting procedures make a difference. In Table 1.1 the difference is, indeed, maximal.

The procedure–dependence of voting outcomes occasionally makes headlines in practical politics as well, although extreme cases akin to Table 1.1 have not been reported. The standard example is the discussion that followed the 2000 presidential election in the United States where the elected president received less popular votes than the runner–up candidate. The same kind of occurrence took place again in the 2016 US presidential election and has happened several times earlier in the electoral history of the United States.

A less known but very important case of demonstrating procedure–dependence is the parliamentary vote taken on 20 June 1991 concerning the location of the central governmental institutions—parliament and the highest level of the executive branch—in Germany after the unification. The outcome, i.e., the re–location of both institutional bodies from Bonn to Berlin, was the result of a relatively complicated agenda of voting and arguably another outcome might well have resulted had a different and less complicated route been followed (see Leininger 1993; Nurmi 2002, pp. 68–71). The Berlin–Bonn example remains somewhat conjectural because, despite Leininger's scrupulous analysis, we do not have complete information about the preference profile of all members of the Bundestag.[1] Yet, it seems quite likely that had the Plurality Voting procedure or Borda count been applied on all suggested decision alternatives, the outcome would have been Bonn as the site of both institutions, while the Condorcet Winner was Berlin, i.e., most systems based on pairwise majority comparisons would have elected Berlin. So, positional and binary voting outcomes would have been different. In practice neither of these procedures as such was followed but the outcome resulted from a mixture of binary systems complicated by the fact that some decision alternatives were withdrawn in the middle of the balloting sequence.

The fact that we have relatively few fully documented instances of downright discrepancy between voting outcomes in a fixed profile of opinions, is due to the paucity of information concerning voter preferences. In parliaments which are typical forums of voting, the full preference rankings of the parliamentarians are not reported. Instead, one has to infer them from the records on pairwise comparisons. The same is true *a fortiori* about voter preferences in general elections.

That different procedures may result in different outcomes motivates the research on the properties of various voting systems. Here the social choice theory has provided the major tools for analysis by suggesting desirable properties (desiderata) that a good voting system should always possess and by devising methods for analyzing preference profiles. Basically the theoretical literature on voting systems can be divided into two main bodies:

1. Research into the compatibility and incompatibility of various desiderata, i.e., into whether the satisfaction of one desideratum makes it possible to satisfy another desideratum under all profiles.
2. Research into whether various voting procedures always satisfy a given desideratum.

This book belongs to the latter genre by focusing on the most obvious desiderata associated with voting procedures, viz., the avoidance of paradoxical outcomes. The study of voting paradoxes is almost as old as the systematic study of voting procedures and many suggested voting procedures can be seen as attempts to avoid specific types of paradoxes. With the present work we aim at reminding social choice theorists, political scientists, as well as commentators, policymakers and interested laymen of the main social–choice properties by which voting procedures for the election of one out of two or more candidates ought to be assessed, and to

[1]The agenda of voting was devised by the Bundesrat, the upper chamber of the German federal parliament, while the voters were members of the lower chamber, the Bundestag.

list, exemplify and explain the (in)vulnerability to various paradoxes of these voting procedures.

Thus this book should be regarded as an updated review by which to assess from a social–choice perspective the main properties of 18 known deterministic voting procedures for the election of a single candidate. As far as we know only three of the procedures (Plurality Voting, Plurality with Runoff, Alternative Vote) are actually used in general public elections, but many of the remaining procedures are used by various public and private organizations when selecting one out of several candidates or alternatives.

The book is organized as follows: In Chap. 2 we survey 13 paradoxes, several of which may afflict any of the 18 voting procedures that are described in Chap. 3. Chapter 4 deals with four voting procedures based on non–ranked voter input and determines their vulnerability or invulnerability to the various voting paradoxes. Chapter 5 assesses the performance of six ranked voting procedures that are not Condorcet extensions in terms of their vulnerability or invulnerability to paradoxes. Chapter 6 turns to eight ranked Condorcet extension procedures providing similar discussion on their performance with respect to the paradoxes. Chapter 7 summarizes and discusses the significance of the results for overall evaluation of voting procedures.

Exercises

Problem 1.1 You are looking for a new bike and, on the basis of extensive study of relevant journals, three models stand out: Bike 1, Bike 2 and Bike 3. There are three bikes stores in your town: A, B and C. None of them has all these bike models. A has Bike 1 and Bike 2, B has Bike 2 and Bike 3 and C has Bike 1 and Bike 3. Suppose that you would prefer Bike 1 in store A, Bike 2 in store B and Bike 3 in store C. Does your choice behavior exhibit transitivity of underlying preferences? If it does, write down the ranking. If it doesn't, which changes are needed to make it transitive?

Problem 1.2 Use now three criteria assumed to be of equal importance to you: price, weight, outlook. Suppose that in comparing any two bike models, your preference is determined by the respective ranking of these two models on a majority of criteria. Can you form a set of rankings over the three bike models with respect to the three criteria so that the resulting preference ranking is intransitive?

Problem 1.3 Construct a 3–voter, 3–alternative Condorcet Paradox. Switch the ranking of any two adjacent alternatives in one ranking. Analyze the ensuing profile: is there still an intransitive majority preference relation? Is there a Condorcet Winner?

Answers to Exercises

Problem 1.1 The answer to the first question: No, it doesn't.
The answer to the second question: Choose Bike 1 in store C.

Problem 1.2 If the preference orderings for bikes (from top to bottom) in terms of the three criteria are as shown in the table below then the resulting ordering is intransitive.

Price	Weight	Outlook
Bike 1	Bike 2	Bike 3
Bike 2	Bike 3	Bike 1
Bike 3	Bike 1	Bike 2

Problem 1.3 Here's a profile constituting a Condorcet Paradox in which the social preference ordering is intransitive ($a \succ b \succ c \succ a$):

No. of voters	Preference ordering
1	$a \succ b \succ c$
1	$b \succ c \succ a$
1	$c \succ a \succ b$

Now switch a and b in the first ranking to get:

No. of voters	Preference ordering
1	$b \succ a \succ c$
1	$b \succ c \succ a$
1	$c \succ a \succ b$

Here the social preference ordering is transitive ($b \succ c \succ a$), i.e., b is the Condorcet Winner.

References

Leininger, W. (1993). The fatal vote: Berlin versus Bonn. *Finanzarchiv, 50,* 1–20.

Nurmi, H. (2002). *Voting procedures under uncertainty*. Berlin, Heidelberg, New York.: Springer Verlag.

Riker, W. H. (1982). *Liberalism against populism: A confrontation between the theory of democracy and the theory of social choice*. San Francisco: W.H. Freeman.

Chapter 2
Voting Paradoxes

Abstract Voting paradoxes pertaining to the election of a single winner are introduced. The paradoxes are divided into five simple paradoxes and eight conditional ones. The simple paradoxes are paradoxes where the relevant data lead to a 'surprising' and arguably undesirable outcome, whereas the conditional paradoxes are ones where the change in one relevant datum while holding constant the other relevant data leads to a 'surprising' and arguably undesirable outcome.

Keywords Simple voting paradoxes · Conditional voting paradoxes

We define a '*voting paradox*' as an undesirable outcome that a voting procedure may produce and which may be regarded at first glance, at least by some people, as surprising or as counter-intuitive.

We distinguish between two types of voting paradoxes associated with a given voting procedure:

1. '*Simple*' or '*Straightforward*' *paradoxes*: These are paradoxes where the relevant data leads to a 'surprising' and arguably undesirable outcome. (The relevant data include, *inter alia*, the number of voters, the number of candidates, the number of candidates that must be elected, the preference ordering of every voter among the competing candidates, the amount of information voters have regarding all other voters' preference orderings, the order in which voters cast their votes if it is not simultaneous, the order in which candidates are voted upon if candidates are not voted upon simultaneously, whether voting is open or secret, and the manner in which ties are to be broken).
2. '*Conditional*' *paradoxes*: These are paradoxes where changing one relevant datum while holding constant all other relevant data leads to a 'surprising' and arguably undesirable outcome.

An array of paradoxes of one or both types are described and analyzed by McGarvey (1953), Riker (1958), Smith (1973), Fishburn (1973, 1974, 1977, 1981,

---

This chapter is largely based on Felsenthal (2012).

D. S. Felsenthal and H. Nurmi, *Voting Procedures for Electing a Single Candidate*, SpringerBriefs in Economics, https://doi.org/10.1007/978-3-319-74033-1_2

1982), Young (1974), Niemi and Riker (1976), Doron and Kronick (1977), Doron (1979), Richelson (1975, 1978a, b, 1979, 1981), Gehrlein (1983), Fishburn and Brams (1983), Saari (1984, 1987, 1989, 1994, 2000, 2001, 2008), Niou (1987), Moulin (1988a), Merlin and Saari (1997), Brams et al. (1998), Scarsini (1998), Nurmi (1998a, b, 1999, 2004, 2007), Lepelley and Merlin (2001), Merlin et al. (2002), Merlin and Valognes (2004), Tideman (1987, 2006), Gehrlein and Lepelley (2011), among others.

2.1 Simple Paradoxes

The five best-known 'simple' paradoxes that may afflict voting procedures designed to elect one out of two or more candidates are the following:

2.1.1 *The Condorcet Winner Paradox (*Condorcet de 1785; Black 1958*)*

A candidate x is not elected despite the fact that it constitutes a 'Condorcet Winner', i.e., despite the fact that x is preferred by a majority of the voters over each of the other competing alternatives.

2.1.2 *The Absolute Majority Winner Paradox*

This is a special case of the Condorcet Winner Paradox. A candidate x may not be elected despite the fact that it is the candidate ranked first by an absolute majority of the voters.

2.1.3 *The Condorcet Loser or Borda Paradox (*Borda de 1784; Black 1958*)*

A candidate x is elected despite the fact that it constitutes a 'Condorcet Loser' i.e., despite the fact that a majority of voters prefer each of the remaining candidates to x. This paradox is a special case of the violation of Smith's (1973) *Condorcet Principle*. According to this principle, if it is possible to partition the set of candidates into two disjoint subsets, A and B, such that each candidate in A is preferred by a majority of the voters over each candidate in B, then no candidate in B ought to be elected unless all candidates in A are elected.

2.1.4 *The Absolute Majority Loser Paradox*

This is a special case of the Condorcet Loser Paradox. A candidate x may be elected despite the fact that it is ranked last by a majority of voters.

2.1.5 *The Pareto (or Dominated Candidate) Paradox* (Fishburn 1974)

A candidate x may be elected while candidate y may not be elected despite the fact that *all* voters prefer candidate y to x.

2.2 Conditional Paradoxes

The eight best-known 'conditional' paradoxes that may afflict voting procedures for electing a single candidate are the following:

2.2.1 *Additional Support (or Lack of Monotonicity or Negative Responsiveness) Paradox* (Smith 1973; Fishburn 1974a; Fishburn and Brams 1983)

If candidate x is elected under a given distribution of voters' preferences among the competing candidates, it is possible that, *ceteris paribus*, x may not be elected if some voter(s) *increase(s) his/her (their) support for* x by moving x to a higher position in his/her (their) preference ordering. Alternatively, if candidate x is not elected under a given distribution of voters' preferences among the competing candidates, it is possible that, *ceteris paribus*, x will be elected if some voter(s) *decrease(s)* his/her (their) support for x by moving x to a lower position in his/her (their) preference ordering.[1]

[1]Another version of the non-monotonicity paradox (which is not demonstrated in this book) is a situation where x is elected in a given electorate but may not be elected if, *ceteris paribus*, additional voters join the electorate who rank x at the top of their preference ordering, or, alternatively, a situation where x is not elected in a given electorate but may be elected if, *ceteris paribus*, additional voters join the electorate who rank x at the bottom of their preference ordering. For this version of non-monotonicity see Felsenthal and Nurmi (2016, 2017).

2.2.2 *Reinforcement (or Inconsistency or Multiple Districts) Paradox* (Young 1974)

If x is elected in each of several disjoint electorates, it is possible that, *ceteris paribus*, x will not be elected if all electorates are combined into a single electorate.

2.2.3 *Truncation Paradox* (Brams 1982; Fishburn and Brams 1983)

A voter may obtain a more preferable outcome if, *ceteris paribus*, s/he lists in his/her ballot only part of his/her (sincere) preference ordering instead of listing his/her entire preference ordering among all the competing candidates.

2.2.4 *No-Show Paradox* (Fishburn and Brams 1983; Ray 1986; Moulin 1988b; Holzman 1988/1989; Perez 1995)

This is an extreme version of the Truncation Paradox. A voter may obtain a more preferable outcome if s/he decides not to participate in an election than, *ceteris paribus*, if s/he decides to participate in the election and vote sincerely for his/her top preference(s). A particular version of this paradox is stated thus: "The addition of identical ballots with candidate x ranked last may change the winner from another candidate to x." (cf. Fishburn and Brams 1983, p. 207).

2.2.5 *Twin Paradox* (Moulin 1988b)

This is a special version of the No-Show Paradox. Two voters having the same preference ordering may obtain a preferable outcome if, *ceteris paribus*, one of them decides not to participate in the election while the other votes sincerely.

2.2.6 *Violation of the Subset Choice Condition (SCC)* (Fishburn 1974b, c; 1977)

SCC requires that when there are at least three candidates and candidate x is the unique winner, then x must not become a loser whenever any of the original losers is removed and all other things remain the same. In the context of individual choice theory SCC is known as Chernoff's condition (1954, p. 429, postulate 4) which states that if an alternative x chosen from a set T is an element of a subset S of T, then x must be chosen also from S. This principle is called 'heritage' by Aizerman and Malishevski (1981, p. 1033) and 'property alpha' by Sen (1970, p. 17).

2.2.7 *Preference Inversion Paradox*

If the individual preferences of each voter are inverted it is possible that, *ceteris paribus,* the (unique) original winner will still win.

2.2.8 *Dependence on Order of Voting (DOV) Paradox* (Farquharson 1969)

If the voting on the competing candidates is conducted sequentially rather than simultaneously, it is possible that candidate x will be elected under a particular sequence but not, *ceteris paribus*, under an alternative sequence.

Exercises

Problem 2.1 Consider the following profile of five voters among five alternatives, a–e:

No. of voters	Preference orderings
1	$a \succ e \succ c \succ b \succ d$
1	$b \succ a \succ d \succ e \succ c$
1	$c \succ a \succ e \succ b \succ d$
1	$a \succ b \succ d \succ e \succ c$
1	$d \succ c \succ a \succ b \succ e$

Are there Pareto-dominated candidates, i.e., such candidates that are ranked lower than some other candidate by *all* voters?

Problem 2.2 What is the largest margin of victory in pairwise comparisons in the above profile?

Problem 2.3 Is there a Condorcet Winner in the above profile? Is there a Condorcet Loser?

Problem 2.4 If there is a Condorcet Winner in the above profile, would s/he gain the plurality of votes (and therefore be elected) if all voters would vote for their top 3 preferences?

Answers to Exercises

Problem 2.1 Candidate *e* is Pareto-dominated by candidate *a*. None of the other candidates can be Pareto-dominated since there is at least one voter that ranks them first.

Problem 2.2 5–0 (*a* vs. *e*)

Problem 2.3 Yes, *a* is the Condorcet Winner. No, there isn't a Condorcet Loser since all candidates defeat at least one other candidate in pairwise contests by a majority of votes.

Problem 2.4 Yes, the Condorcet Winner (*a*) would be elected since *a* would receive more votes (5) than any of the other alternatives.

References

Aizerman, M. A., & Malishevski, A. V. (1981). General theory of best variants choice: Some aspects. *IEEE Transactions on Automatic Control AC–26,* 1030–1040.

Black, D. (1958). *The theory of committees and elections.* Cambridge: Cambridge University Press.

Borda, J.C. de (1784) [1995]. Mémoire sur les élections au scrutin, *Histoire de l'Academie Royale des Sciences année* 1781 (pp. 651–665). Paris. Reprinted and translated in I. McLean and A. B. Urken (1995), *Classics of social choice* (pp. 83–89). Ann Arbor, MI: University of Michigan Press.

Brams, S. J. (1982). The AMS nominating system is vulnerable to truncation of preferences. *Notices of the American Mathematical Society, 29,* 136–138.

Brams, S. J., Kilgour, D. M., & Zwicker, W. S. (1998). The paradox of multiple elections. *Social Choice and Welfare, 15,* 211–236.

Chernoff, H. (1954). Rational selection of decision functions. *Econometrica, 22,* 422–443.

Condorcet, M. de (1785). *Essai sur l'application de l'analyse à la probabilité des décisions rendues à la pluralité des voix.* Paris: L'Imprimerie Royale.

Doron, G. (1979). The Hare voting system is inconsistent. *Political Studies, 27,* 283–286.

Doron, G., & Kronick, R. (1977). Single transferable vote: An example of a perverse social choice function. *American Journal of Political Science, 21,* 303–311.

Farquharson, R. (1969). *Theory of voting*. New Haven, CT: Yale University Press.

Felsenthal, D. S. (2012). Review of paradoxes afflicting procedures for electing a single candidate. In D. S. Felsenthal & M. Machover (Eds.), *Electoral systems: Paradoxes, assumptions, and procedures* (pp. 19–92). Berlin: Springer (Ch. 3).

Felsenthal, D. S., & Nurmi, H. (2016). Two types of participation failure under nine voting methods in variable electorates. *Public Choice, 168,* 115–135.

Felsenthal, D. S., & Nurmi, H. (2017). *Monotonicity failures afflicting procedures for electing a single candidate.* Cham, Switzerland: Springer.

Fishburn, P. C. (1973). *The theory of social choice*. Princeton, NJ: Princeton University Press.

Fishburn, P. C. (1974). Paradoxes of voting. *American Political Science Review, 68,* 537–546.

Fishburn, P. C. (1974a). Social choice functions. *SIAM Review, 16,* 63–90.

Fishburn, P. C. (1974b). On the sum-of-ranks winner when losers are removed. *Discrete Mathematics, 8,* 25–30.

Fishburn, P. C. (1974c). Subset choice conditions and the computation of social choice sets. *The Quarterly Journal of Economics, 88,* 320–329.

Fishburn, P. C. (1977). Condorcet social choice functions. *SIAM Journal on Applied Mathematics, 33,* 469–489.

Fishburn, P. C. (1981). Inverted orders for monotone scoring rules. *Discrete Applied Mathematics, 3,* 27–36.

Fishburn, P. C. (1982). Monotonicity paradoxes in the theory of elections. *Discrete Applied Mathematics, 4,* 119–134.

Fishburn, P. C., & Brams, S. J. (1983). Paradoxes of preferential voting. *Mathematics Magazine, 56,* 207–214.

Gehrlein, W. V. (1983). Condorcet's paradox. *Theory and Decision, 15,* 161–197.

Gehrlein, W. V., & Lepelley, D. (2011). *Voting paradoxes and group coherence: The Condorcet efficiency of voting rules*. Berlin: Springer.

Holzman, R. (1988/1989). To vote or not to vote: What is the quota? *Discrete Applied Mathematics, 22,* 133–141.

Lepelley, D., & Merlin, V. (2001). Scoring runoff paradoxes for variable electorates. *Economic Theory, 17,* 53–80.

McGarvey, D. C. (1953). A theorem on the construction of voting paradoxes. *Econometrica, 21,* 608–610.

Merlin, V. R., & Saari, D. G. (1997). The Copeland method II: Manipulation, monotonicity and paradoxes. *Journal of Economic Theory, 72,* 148–172.

Merlin, V., & Valognes, F. (2004). The impact of indifferent voters on the likelihood of some voting paradoxes. *Mathematical Social Sciences, 48,* 343–361.

Merlin, V., Tataru, M., & Valognes, F. (2002). The likelihood of Condorcet's profiles. *Social Choice and Welfare, 19,* 193–206.

Moulin, H. (1988a). *Axioms of cooperative decision making*. Cambridge: Cambridge University Press.

Moulin, H. (1988b). Condorcet's principle implies the No–Show paradox. *Journal of Economic Theory, 45,* 53–64.

Niemi, R. G., & Riker, W. H. (1976). The choice of voting systems. *Scientific American, 234,* 21–27.

Niou, E. M. S. (1987). A note on Nanson's rule. *Public Choice, 54,* 191–193.

Nurmi, H. (1998a). *Rational behavior and the design of institutions: Concepts, theories and models*. Cheltenham: Edward Elgar.

Nurmi, H. (1998b). Voting paradoxes and referenda. *Social Choice and Welfare, 15,* 333–350.

Nurmi, H. (1999). *Voting paradoxes and how to deal with them*. Berlin, New York: Springer.

Nurmi, H. (2004). A comparison of some distance-based choice rules in ranking environments. *Theory and Decision, 57,* 5–23.

Nurmi, H. (2007). Assessing Borda's rule and its modifications. In P. Emerson (Ed.), *Designing an all–inclusive democracy: Consensual voting procedures for use in parliaments, councils and committees* (pp. 109–119). Berlin: Springer (Ch. 6).

Pérez, J. (1995). Incidence of No–Show paradoxes in Condorcet choice functions. *Investigaciones Economicas, 19,* 139–154.

Ray, D. (1986). On the practical possibility of a 'No–Show paradox' under the single transferable vote. *Mathematical Social Sciences, 11,* 183–189.

Richelson, J. T. (1975). A comparative analysis of social choice functions. *Behavioral Science, 20,* 331–337.

Richelson, J. T. (1978a). A comparative analysis of social choice functions, II. *Behavioral Science, 23,* 38–44.

Richelson, J. T. (1978b). A comparative analysis of social choice functions, III. *Behavioral Science, 23,* 169–176.

Richelson, J. T. (1979). A comparative analysis of social choice functions I, II, III: A summary. *Behavioral Science, 24,* 355.

Richelson, J. T. (1981). A comparative analysis of social choice functions, IV. *Behavioral Science, 26,* 346–353.
Riker, W. H. (1958). The paradox of voting and Congressional rules for voting on amendments. *American Political Science Review, 52,* 349–366.
Saari, D. G. (1984). The ultimate of chaos resulting from weighted voting systems. *Advances in Applied Mathematics, 5,* 286–308.
Saari, D. G. (1987). The source of some paradoxes from social choice and probability. *Journal of Economic Theory, 41,* 1–22.
Saari, D. G. (1989). A dictionary for voting paradoxes. *Journal of Economic Theory, 48,* 443–475.
Saari, D. G. (1994). *Geometry of voting*. New York: Springer.
Saari, D. G. (2000). Mathematical structure of voting paradoxes. *Economic Theory, 15,* 1–53, 55–102.
Saari, D. G. (2001). *Chaotic elections! A mathematician looks at voting*. Providence, RI: American Mathematical Society.
Saari, D. G. (2008). *Disposing dictators, demystifying voting paradoxes: Social choice analysis*. New York: Cambridge University Press.
Scarsini, M. (1998). A strong paradox of multiple elections. *Social Choice and Welfare, 15,* 237–238.
Sen, A. K. (1970). *Collective choice and social welfare*. San Francisco: Holden-Day.
Smith, J. H. (1973). Aggregation of preferences with variable electorate. *Econometrica, 41,* 1027–1041.
Tideman, T. N. (1987). Independence of clones as a criterion for voting rules. *Social Choice and Welfare, 4,* 185–206.
Tideman, N. (2006). *Collective decisions and voting: The potential for public choice*. Aldershot, Hampshire, England: Ashgate Publishing Ltd.
Young, H. P. (1974). An axiomatization of Borda's rule. *Journal of Economic Theory, 9,* 43–52.

Chapter 3
Voting Procedures Designed to Elect a Single Candidate

Abstract 18 voting procedures for electing a single candidate are introduced and briefly commented upon. The procedures fall into three classes in terms of the type of voter input and Condorcet consistency: non–ranked procedures, ranked procedures that are not Condorcet–consistent and ranked ones that are Condorcet–consistent. The first class consists of four procedures, the second consists of six procedures and the third class consists of eight procedures.

Keywords Non–ranked voting procedures · Ranked procedures · Condorcet–consistent procedures

3.1 Non–Ranked Voting Procedures

There are four main voting procedures for electing a single candidate where voters do not have to rank–order the candidates.

3.1.1 Plurality Voting (aka First Past the Post) Procedure

This is the most common procedure for electing a single candidate, and is used, *inter alia*, for electing the members of the House of Commons in the UK and the members of the House of Representatives in the US. Under this procedure every voter casts one vote for a single candidate and the candidate obtaining the largest number of votes is elected.

This chapter is largely based on Felsenthal (2012).

D. S. Felsenthal and H. Nurmi, *Voting Procedures for Electing a Single Candidate*, SpringerBriefs in Economics, https://doi.org/10.1007/978-3-319-74033-1_3

3.1.2 *Plurality with Runoff Voting Procedure*

Under the usual version of this procedure up to two voting rounds are conducted. In the first round each voter casts one vote for a single candidate. In order to win in the first round a candidate must obtain either a special plurality (usually at least 40% of the votes) or an absolute majority of the votes. If no candidate is declared the winner in the first round then a second round is conducted. In this round only the two candidates who obtained the highest number of votes in the first round participate, and the one who obtains the majority of votes wins. This too is a very common procedure for electing a single candidate and it is currently used for electing the President in 40 countries, *inter alia*, in Argentina, Austria, Brazil, Finland, France, India, Portugal, Romania, Russia, Turkey and Ukraine. In France it is also used to elect the members of the legislature, and in Israel it is used to elect mayors and was used to elect the Prime Minister in the 1996, 1999, and 2001 elections.

This procedure can also be viewed as a procedure where voters rank–order all the competing alternatives and visit the ballot box only once—but there are up to two counting rounds. If in the first counting round there exists an alternative which is ranked first by an absolute majority of the voters then this alternative is declared the winner. But if no alternative is ranked first by an absolute majority of the voters then: (1) one selects the two alternatives which received more votes in the first count than each of the other alternatives; suppose these are alternatives x and y. (2) One then inspects all ballots where neither x nor y were listed first to determine in how many of these ballots x is preferred to y and in how many y is preferred to x. These numbers are then added to the number of ballots in which x and y were listed first to determine the ultimate winner.

3.1.3 *Approval Voting (***Brams and Fishburn 1978, 1983***)*

Under this procedure every voter has a number of votes which is equal to the number of competing candidates, and every voter can cast one vote or no vote for every candidate. The candidate obtaining the largest number of votes is elected. So far this procedure has not been used in any public elections but is already used by several professional associations and universities in electing their officers.

3.1.4 *Successive Elimination (***Farquharson 1969***)*

This procedure is common in parliaments when voting on alternative versions of bills. According to this procedure voting is conducted in a series of rounds. In each round two alternatives compete; the one obtaining fewer votes is eliminated and the other competes in the next round against one of the alternatives which has not yet been eliminated. The alternative winning in the last round is the ultimate winner.

3.2 Ranked Voting Procedures that are not Condorcet-Consistent

Six ranked procedures under which every voter must rank-order all competing candidates—but which do not ensure the election of a Condorcet Winner when one exists—have been proposed, as far as we know, during the last 250 years. These procedures are described below. Only one of these procedures (Alternative Vote) is used currently in public elections.

3.2.1 *Borda's Count* (Borda 1784; Black 1958)

This voting procedure was proposed by Jean Charles de Borda in a paper he delivered in 1770 before the French Royal Academy of Sciences entitled 'Memorandum on election by ballot' ('Mémoire sur les élections au scrutin'). According to Borda's procedure each candidate, x, is given a score equal to the sum of voters who prefer x to each of the other alternatives, and the candidate with the largest score is elected. Thus the Borda winner can be viewed also as the candidate who occupies the highest position, *on average*, in the rankings of the voters. Equivalently, under Borda's procedure each candidate x gets no points for each voter who ranks x last in his/her preference ordering, 1 point for each voter who ranks x second-to-last in his/her preference ordering, and so on, and $n-1$ points for each voter who ranks x first in his/her preference ordering (where n is the number of candidates). The candidate with the largest number of points is elected. Thus if all v voters have linear preference orderings among the n candidates then the total number of points obtained by all candidates is equal to the number of voters multiplied by the number of paired comparisons among the candidates, i.e., to $vn(n-1)/2$.

3.2.2 *Alternative Vote (aka Instant Runoff)*

This is the version of the *Single Transferable Vote* (STV) procedure (independently proposed by Carl George Andrae in Denmark in 1855 and by Thomas Hare in England in 1857) for electing a single candidate. It works as follows. In the first step one verifies whether there exists a candidate who is ranked first by an absolute majority of the voters. If such a candidate exists s/he is declared the winner. If no such candidate exists then, in the second step, the candidate who is ranked first by the smallest number of voters is deleted from all ballots and thereafter one again verifies whether there is now a candidate who is ranked first by an absolute majority of the voters. The elimination process continues in this way until a candidate who is ranked first by an absolute majority of the voters is found. The Alternative Vote procedure is used in electing the President of the Republic of Ireland, the Australian House of Representatives, as well as the mayors in some municipal elections in the US.

3.2.3 *Coombs' Method* (Coombs 1964, pp. 397–399; Straffin 1980; Coombs et al. 1984)

This procedure was proposed by the psychologist Clyde H. Coombs in 1964. It is similar to Alternative Vote except that the elimination in a given round under Coombs' method involves the candidate who is ranked last by the largest number of voters (instead of the candidate who is ranked first by the smallest number of voters under Alternative Vote).

3.2.4 *Bucklin's Method* (Hoag and Hallett 1926, pp. 485–491; Tideman 2006, p. 203)

This voting system can be used for single–member and multi–member district elections. It is named after James W. Bucklin of Grand Junction, Colorado, who first promoted it in 1909. In 1913 the US Congress prescribed (in the Federal Reserve Act of 1913, Section 4) that this method be used for electing district directors of each Federal Reserve Bank.

Under Bucklin's method voters rank–order the competing candidates. The vote count starts like in the Alternative Vote method. If there exists a candidate who is ranked first by an absolute majority of the voters s/he is elected. Otherwise the number of voters who ranked every candidate in second place are added to the number of voters who ranked him/her first, and if now there exists a candidate supported by a majority of voters s/he is elected. If not, the counting process continues in this way by adding for each candidate his/her third, fourth, …, and so forth rankings, until a candidate is found who is supported by an absolute majority of the voters. If two or more candidates are found to be supported by a majority of voters in the same counting round then the one supported by the largest majority is elected.[1]

3.2.5 *Range Voting* (Smith 2000)

According to this procedure the suitability (or level of performance) of every candidate is assessed by every voter and is assigned a (cardinal) grade (chosen from a pre–specified range) reflecting the candidate's suitability or level of performance in the eyes of the voter. The candidate with the highest average grade is the winner. This procedure is currently championed by Warren D. Smith (see http://rangevoting.org) and used to elect the winner in various sport competitions.

3.2.6 *Majority Judgment* (Balinski and Laraki 2007a, b, 2011)

According to this proposed procedure, the suitability (or level of performance) of every candidate is assessed by every voter and is assigned an ordinal grade (chosen from a pre–specified range) reflecting the candidate's suitability or level of performance in the eyes of the voter. The candidate with the highest median grade is the winner.

[1]However, it is unclear how a tie between two candidates, say a and b, ought to be broken under Bucklin's procedure when both a and b are supported in the same counting round by the same number of voters and this number constitutes a majority of the voters. If one tries to break the tie between a and b in such an eventuality by performing the next counting round in which all other candidates are also allowed to participate, then it is possible that the number of (cumulated) votes of another candidate, c, will exceed that of a and b.

To see this, consider the following simple example. Suppose there are 18 voters who must elect one candidate under Bucklin's procedure and whose preference orderings among four candidates, a, b, c, d are as follows: seven voters with preference ordering $a \succ b \succ c \succ d$, eight voters with preference ordering $b \succ a \succ c \succ d$, one voter with preference ordering $d \succ c \succ a \succ b$, and two voters with preference ordering $d \succ c \succ b \succ a$. None of the candidates constitutes the top preference of a majority of the voters. However, both a and b constitute the top or second preference by a majority of voters (15). If one tries to break the tie between a and b by performing the next (third) counting round in which c and d are also allowed to participate, then c will be elected (with 18 votes), but if only a and b are allowed to participate in this counting round then b will be elected (with 17 votes).

So which candidate ought to be elected in this example under Bucklin's procedure? As far as we know, Bucklin did not supply an answer to this question.

3.3 Ranked Voting Procedures that are Condorcet–Consistent[2]

All the eight voting procedures described in this section require that voters rank–order all competing candidates. Under all these procedures a Condorcet Winner, if one exists, is elected. The procedures differ from one another regarding which candidate gets elected when a Condorcet Winner does not exist.

3.3.1 The Minimax Procedure

Condorcet specified that the Condorcet Winner (whom he called 'the majority candidate') ought to be elected if one exists. However, according to Black (1958, pp. 174–175, 187) Condorcet did not specify clearly which candidate ought to be elected when the *social preference ordering*[3] contains a top cycle. Black (1958, p. 175) suggests that "It would be most in accordance with the spirit of Condorcet's … analysis … to discard all candidates except those with the minimum number of majorities against them and then to deem the largest size of minority to be a majority, and so on, until one candidate had only actual or deemed majorities against each of the others." In other words, the procedure attributed by Black to Condorcet when cycles exist in the social preference ordering is a *Minimax procedure*[4] since it chooses that candidate whose worst loss in the paired comparisons is the least bad. This procedure is also known in the literature as the *Simpson–Kramer rule* (see Simpson 1969; Kramer 1977).

3.3.2 Dodgson's Procedure (Black 1958, pp. 222–234; McLean and Urken, 1995, pp. 288–297)

This procedure is named after the Rev. Charles Lutwidge Dodgson, aka Lewis Carroll, who proposed it in 1876. It elects the Condorcet Winner when one exists. If

---

[2]We list here only deterministic procedures. For a Condorcet–consistent probabilistic procedure see, for example, Felsenthal and Machover (1992). We also do not list here two Condorcet–consistent deterministic procedures proposed by Tideman (1987) and by Schulze (2003) because we do not consider satisfying (or violating) the independence–of–clones property, which is the main reason why these two procedures were proposed, to be associated with any voting paradox. (A phenomenon where candidate x is more likely to be elected when two clone candidates, y and y', exist, and where x is less likely to be elected when, *ceteris paribus*, one of the clone candidates withdraws, does not seem to us surprising or counter–intuitive). Except for Black's (1958) hybrid procedure, which is well–known, we do not analyze any other hybrid procedure.

[3]This is the preference ordering of the majority of the voters and it may not be unique because different majorities of voters may have different preference orderings.

[4]Young (1977, p. 349) prefers to call this procedure 'The Minimax function'.

no Condorcet Winner exists it elects that candidate who requires the fewest number of switches (i.e., inversions of two adjacent candidates) in the voters' preference orderings in order to make him or her the Condorcet Winner.

3.3.3 *Nanson's Method* (Nanson 1883; McLean and Urken 1995, Ch. 14)

Nanson's method is a recursive elimination of Borda's method. In the first step one calculates for each candidate his/her Borda score. In the second step the candidates whose Borda score does not exceed the average Borda score of the candidates in the first step are eliminated from all ballots and revised Borda scores are computed for the remaining candidates. The elimination process is continued in this way until one candidate is left. If a (strong) Condorcet Winner exists then Nanson's method elects him/her.[5]

3.3.4 *Copeland's Method* (Copeland 1951)

Every candidate x gets one point for every paired comparison with another candidate y in which an absolute majority of the voters prefer x to y, and half a point for every paired comparison in which the number of voters preferring x to y is equal to the number of voters preferring y to x. The candidate obtaining the largest sum of points is the winner.

3.3.5 *Black's Method* (Black 1958, p. 66)

According to this method one first performs all paired comparisons to verify whether a Condorcet Winner exists. If such a winner exists then s/he is elected. Otherwise the winner according to the Borda count (see above) is elected.

---

[5]Although Nanson's procedure satisfies the strong Condorcet condition, i.e., it always elects a candidate who beats every other candidate in paired comparisons, this procedure may not satisfy the weak Condorcet condition which requires that if there exist(s) candidate(s) who is (are) unbeaten by any other candidate then this (these) candidate(s)—and only this (these) candidate(s)—ought to be elected. For an example of violation of the weak Condorcet condition by Nanson's procedure see Niou (1987). Niou shows that when the set of Nanson winners consists of two candidates, one of them may not satisfy the weak Condorcet condition, while the other Nanson winner does. The following profile (where the symbol $\succ$ means "is preferred to") shows that the Nanson winner may be distinct from those candidates that satisfy the weak Condorcet condition (Nurmi 1989, p. 202): one voter: $a \succ b \succ c \succ d \succ e$, one voter: $a \succ d \succ b \succ c \succ e$, one voter: $a \succ d \succ e \succ b \succ c$, one voter: $b \succ c \succ e \succ d \succ a$, two voters: $c \succ e \succ d \succ b \succ a$. Here the Nanson winner is c, but the only candidate satisfying the weak Condorcet condition is a.

3.3.6 *Kemeny's Method* (Kemeny 1959; Kemeny and Snell 1960; Young and Levenglick 1978; Young 1988, 1995)

Kemeny's method (aka *Kemeny–Young rule*) specifies that up to $n!$ possible social preference orderings should be examined (where n is the number of candidates) in order to determine which of these is the "most likely" true social preference ordering.[6] The selected "most likely" social preference ordering according to this method is the one where the number of pairs (V, y), where V is a voter and y is a candidate such that V prefers x to y, and y is ranked below x in the social preference ordering is maximized. Given the voters' various preference orderings, Kemeny's procedure can also be viewed as finding the most likely (or the best predictor, or the best compromise) true social preference ordering, called the *median preference ordering*, i.e., that social preference ordering S that minimizes the sum, over all voters i, of the number of pairs of candidates that are ordered oppositely by S and by the ith voter.[7]

3.3.7 *Schwartz's Method* (Schwartz 1972, 1986)

Thomas Schwartz's method is based on the notion that a candidate x deserves to be listed ahead of another candidate y in the social preference ordering if and only if x beats or ties with some candidate that beats y, and x beats or ties with all candidates that y beats or ties with. The Schwartz set (from which the winner should be chosen) is the smallest set of candidates who are unbeatable by candidates outside the set. The Schwartz set is also called *GOCHA* (*Generalized Optimal Choice Axiom*).

[6]Tideman (2006, pp. 187–189) proposes two heuristic procedures that simplify the need to examine all $n!$ preference orderings.

[7]According to Kemeny (1959) the distance between two preference orderings, R and R', is the number of pairs of candidates (alternatives) on which they differ. For example, if $R = a \succ b \succ c \succ d$ and $R' = d \succ a \succ b \succ c$, then the distance between R and R' is 3, because they agree on three pairs $[(a \succ b), (a \succ c), (b \succ c)]$ but differ on the remaining three pairs, i.e., on the preference ordering between a and d, b and d, and between c and d. Similarly, if R'' is $c \succ d \succ a \succ b$ then the distance between R and R'' is 4 and the distance between R' and R'' is 3. According to Kemeny's procedure the most likely social preference ordering is that R such that the sum of distances of the voters' preference orderings from R is minimized. Because this R has the properties of the median central measure in statistics it is called the *median preference ordering*. The median preference ordering (but not the *mean preference ordering* which is that R which minimizes the sum of the squared differences between R and the voters' preference orderings) will be identical to the possible social preference ordering W which maximizes the sum of voters that agree with all paired comparisons implied by W.

3.3.8 *Young's Method* (Young 1977)

According to Fishburn's (1977, p. 473) informal description of Young's procedure "[it] is like Dodgson's in the sense that it is based on altered profiles that have candidates who lose to no other candidate under simple majority. But unlike Dodgson, Young deletes voters rather than inverting preferences to obtain the altered profiles. His procedure suggests that we remain most faithful to Condorcet's Principle if the choice set consists of alternatives that can become simple majority non–losers with removal of the fewest number of voters."

Exercises

Problem 3. 1 Consider the following profile:

No. of voters	Preference ordering
5	$a \succ c \succ b \succ d$
4	$b \succ d \succ a \succ c$
2	$c \succ d \succ a \succ b$

Determine the winners according to Bucklin's, Minimax, Plurality with Runoff, and Copeland's procedures.

Problem 3.2 Consider the following profile:

No. of voters	Preference orderings
10	$d \succ a \succ b \succ c$
7	$b \succ c \succ a \succ d$
7	$c \succ a \succ b \succ d$
4	$d \succ c \succ a \succ b$
1	$b \succ a \succ c \succ d$

Determine the winners according to Dodgson's, Minimax, Nanson's, and Kemeny's procedures.

Answers to Exercises

Problem 3.1 The Bucklin Winner is c (on the second round of computing with 7 voters placing it either first or second);

The Minimax Winner is a (with a maximum of 6 votes against it);

The Plurality with Runoff Winner is a (in the runoff with b);

The Copeland Winners are a and c (each defeats two other candidates).

Problem 3.2 The winner according to Dodgson's procedure is d (needing just 3 preference inversions to become a Condorcet Winner);

The Minimax winner is also d whose maximal loss (15) is smallest;

The winner according to Nanson's procedure is c (which beats a 18:11 in the second count);

The most likely (transitive) social preference orderings according to Kemeny are $a \succ b \succ c \succ d$ and $c \succ a \succ b \succ d$ (each supported by the largest number (95) of pairs fitting these social preference orderings), so here according to Kemeny there is a tie between a and c.

References

Balinski, M., & Laraki, R. (2007a). A theory of measuring, electing and ranking. In *Proceedings of the National Academy of Sciences of the United States of America (PNAS)*, 104, 8720–8725.

Balinski, M., & Laraki, R. (2007b). Election by majority judgement: Experimental evidence, (mimeograph). Paris: Ecole Polytechnique, Centre National De La Recherche Scientifique, Laboratoire D'Econometrie, Cahier No. 2007–28. Downoladable from http://tinyurl.com/65q6cg.

Balinski, M., & Laraki, R. (2011). *Majority judgment: Measuring, ranking, and electing*. Cambridge, MA: MIT Press.

Black, D. (1958). *The theory of committees and elections*. Cambridge: Cambridge University Press.

Borda, J.-C. de (1784) [1995]. Mémoire sur les élections au scrutin, *Histoire de l'Academie Royale des Sciences année* 1781, pp. 651–665. Paris. Reprinted and translated in I. McLean and A. B. Urken (1995), *Classics of social choice*, Ann Arbor, MI: University of Michigan Press, pp. 83–89.

Brams, S. J., & Fishburn, P. C. (1978). Approval voting. *American Political Science Review, 72*, 831–847.

Brams, S. J., & Fishburn, P. C. (1983). *Approval voting*. Boston: Birkhäuser.

Coombs, C. H. (1964). *A theory of data*. New York: Wiley.

Coombs, C. H., Cohen, J. L., & Chamberlin, J. R. (1984). An empirical study of some election systems. *American Psychologist, 39*, 140–157.

Copeland, A. H. (1951). A 'reasonable' social welfare function, *mimeographed*. University of Michigan, Department of Mathematics, Seminar on Applications of Mathematics to the Social Sciences.

Farquharson, R. (1969). *Theory of voting*. New Haven, CT: Yale University Press.

Felsenthal, D. S. (2012). Review of paradoxes afflicting procedures for electing a single candidate. In D. S. Felsenthal & M. Machover (Eds.), *Electoral systems: Paradoxes, assumptions, and procedures*. Berlin Heidelberg: Springer, Ch. 3, pp. 19–92.

Felsenthal, D. S., & Machover, M. (1992). After two centuries should Condorcet's voting procedure be implemented? *Behavioral Science, 37,* 250–273.

Fishburn, P. C. (1977). Condorcet social choice functions. *SIAM Journal on Applied Mathematics, 33,* 469–489.

Hoag, C. G., & Hallett, G. H. (1926). *Proportional representation*. New York: The Macmillan Co.

Kemeny, J. G. (1959). Mathematics without numbers. *Daedalus, 88,* 577–591.

Kemeny, J.G., & Snell, J.L. (1960). *Mathematical models in the social sciences*. Boston: Ginn.

Kramer, G. H. (1977). A dynamical model of political equilibrium. *Journal of Economic Theory, 16,* 310–333.

McLean, I., & Urken, A. B. (1995). *Classics of social choice*. Ann Arbor: University of Michigan Press.

Nanson, E. J. (1883). Methods of elections. *Transactions and Proceedings of the Royal Society of Victoria, 19,* 197–240. Also in: Iain McLean and Arnold B. Urken (Eds.), *Classics of social choice.* University of Michigan Press, 1995, Ch. 14, pp. 321–359.

Niou, E. M. S. (1987). A note on Nanson's rule. *Public Choice, 54,* 191–193.

Nurmi, H. (1989). On Nanson's method. In O. Borg, O. Apunen, H. Hakovirta & J. Paastela (Eds.), *Democracy in the modern world. Essays for Tatu Vanhanen.* (Series A, Vol. 260, pp. 199-210). Tampere: Acta Universitatis Tamperensis.

Schultze, M. (2003). A new monotonic and clone–independent single–winner election method. *Voting Counts, 17,* 9–19. (Downloadable from: http://www.macdougall.org.uk/VM/ISSUE17/I17P3.PDF.

Schwartz, T. (1972). Rationality and the myth of the maximum. *Noûs, 6,* 97–117.

Schwartz, T. (1986). *The logic of collective choice.* New York: Columbia University Press.

Simpson, P. B. (1969). On defining areas of voter choice: Professor Tullock on stable voting. *Quarterly Journal of Economics, 83,* 478–490.

Smith, W. D. (2000). *Range Voting*. Downloadable from: http://www.math.temple.edu/~wds/homepage/rangevote.pdf.

Straffin, Ph. D. (1980). *Topics in the theory of voting*. Boston: Birkhäuser.

Tideman, T. N. (1987). Independence of clones as a criterion for voting rules. *Social Choice and Welfare, 4,* 185–206.

Tideman, N. (2006). *Collective decisions and voting: The potential for public choice*. Aldershot, Hampshire, England: Ashgate Publishing Ltd.

Young, H. P. (1977). Extending Condorcet's rule. *Journal of Economic Theory, 16,* 335–353.

Young, H. P. (1988). Condorcet's theory of voting. *American Political Science Review, 82,* 1231–1244.

Young, H. P. (1995). Optimal voting rules. *Journal of Economic Perspectives, 9*(1), 51–63.

Young, H. P., & Levenglick, A. (1978). A consistent extension of Condorcet's election principle. *SIAM Journal of Applied Mathematics, 35,* 283–300.

Chapter 4
The (In)Vulnerability of Non-Ranked Voting Procedures to Various Paradoxes

Abstract Focusing on four procedures that do not require the voters to submit full preference rankings over candidates (Plurality Voting, Plurality with Runoff, Approval Voting, and Successive Elimination), we discuss, for each procedure, those voting paradoxes to which the procedures are immune and the reasons for this, as well as demonstrate, with the aid of illustrative examples, their vulnerability to other paradoxes.

Keywords Vulnerability to paradoxes · Non-ranked voting procedures · Proving by counterexample

4.1 The (In)Vulnerability of the Plurality Voting Procedure to Various Paradoxes

4.1.1 The Condorcet Winner, the Condorcet Loser, the Absolute Majority Loser, the Preference Inversion, and the SCC Paradoxes

The Plurality Voting procedure is vulnerable to these five paradoxes. The following example demonstrates the vulnerability of the Plurality Voting procedure to all these paradoxes simultaneously.

This chapter is partly based on Felsenthal (2012) which contains several examples devised by the second-named author.

Except for the Successive Elimination procedure all other voting procedures surveyed in this chapter are invulnerable to the Dependence on Order of Voting (DOV) Paradox (cf. Sect. 2.2.8 in Chap. 2) because under these procedures all candidates are voted upon simultaneously rather than sequentially.

D. S. Felsenthal and H. Nurmi, *Voting Procedures for Electing a Single Candidate*, SpringerBriefs in Economics, https://doi.org/10.1007/978-3-319-74033-1_4

4.1.1.1 Example

Suppose there are 9 voters who must elect one out of three candidates, *a, b,* and *c,* and whose preference orderings among these candidates are as follows:

No. of voters	Preference orderings
4	$a \succ b \succ c$
3	$b \succ c \succ a$
2	$c \succ b \succ a$

Here *b* is the Condorcet Winner and *a* is not only a Condorcet Loser but also an Absolute Majority Loser. Nevertheless, if all voters vote for their top preference then *a* will be elected. Note that if *c* drops out of the race then *b* will be elected—thus demonstrating the violation of SCC. Note also that if all voters invert their preference orderings then *a* becomes an Absolute Majority Winner and hence will be elected—thus demonstrating the Preference Inversion Paradox.

4.1.2 Absolute Majority Winner Paradox

The Plurality Voting procedure is not susceptible to this paradox because, by definition, it elects the alternative which is supported by the plurality of voters. So when there is a candidate ranked first by an absolute majority, it is *a fortiori* the only one winning by a plurality of votes and hence is the Plurality Voting winner.

4.1.3 Pareto-Dominated Candidate Paradox

The Plurality Voting procedure cannot elect a Pareto-dominated candidate because it elects, by definition, the candidate who is supported by the plurality of voters. So if candidate *x* is Pareto-dominated by some other candidate *y*, then *x* cannot be ranked ahead of *y* by any voter. Hence if no voter votes for a less preferred alternative if s/he can vote for a more preferred alternative then *x* gets no votes at all, and therefore cannot be elected under the Plurality Voting procedure.

4.1.4 Lack of Monotonicity Paradox

The Plurality Voting procedure is not susceptible to lack of monotonicity since increasing candidate *x*'s support, *ceteris paribus*, will keep the number of *x*'s votes the same as originally or increase it, while no other candidate gets more votes. Thus, *x* remains the winner under the Plurality Voting procedure in a fixed electorate. In a variable electorate obtained by adding some voters ranking x first (and voting for x), the vote sums of all other candidates remain the same, but the number of x's votes increases by the number of the added voters. Hence x remains the winner under the Plurality Voting procedure with a larger margin than originally. So, both in fixed and variable electorates additional support for the winner, *ceteris paribus*, maintains its status as the winner under the Plurality Voting procedure.

4.1.5 Reinforcement Paradox

The Plurality Voting procedure is not vulnerable to the Reinforcement Paradox because it always elects the alternative which received the plurality of votes by any given electorate. Hence if two disjoint electorates—each of which awarded x the plurality of votes—are amalgamated into a single electorate then x will receive also the plurality of votes in the amalgamated electorate and hence will be elected by the Plurality Voting procedure.

4.1.6 No-Show Paradox

The Plurality Voting procedure is not vulnerable to the No-Show Paradox since the selected alternative, say x, which by definition is ranked first by the plurality of voters, can be changed to another winner, say y, only if some voters originally ranking x first, abstain. This is because the abstaining of any other voters only increases x's plurality margin. Also those originally ranking x first cannot benefit from abstaining since thereby they decrease x's plurality count, possibly even rendering x a non-winner. Thus, no voters can benefit from abstaining under the Plurality Voting procedure.

4.1.7 Truncation Paradox

This paradox is irrelevant to the Plurality Voting procedure because under this procedure voters do not rank-order the alternatives.

4.1.8 Twin Paradox

The Plurality Voting procedure is invulnerable to the Twin Paradox. On the contrary, the more voters having the same preferences will vote for the same alternative, the more likely will this alternative be selected by the Plurality Voting procedure.

4.2 The (In)Vulnerability of the Plurality with Runoff Procedure to Various Paradoxes

4.2.1 The Condorcet Winner, Lack of Monotonicity, and the SCC Paradoxes

Example 4.2.1.1 below demonstrates the vulnerability of the Plurality with Runoff procedure to these three paradoxes.

4.2.1.1 Example

Suppose there are 43 voters whose preference orderings among three candidates, *a*, *b*, and *c*, are as follows:

No. of voters	Preference orderings
7	$a \succ b \succ c$
9	$a \succ c \succ b$
14	$b \succ c \succ a$
13	$c \succ a \succ b$

Here the pairwise majority comparisons yield that the social preference ordering is $c \succ a \succ b$, i.e., *c* is the Condorcet Winner. But if all voters vote sincerely then under the Plurality with Runoff procedure *c* will be eliminated in the first round and *a* will beat *b* in the second round thus becoming the ultimate winner. Note that if *b* would have withdrawn from the race prior to the first round then, *ceteris paribus*, *c* would have been elected already in the first round, thereby demonstrating this procedure's vulnerability to SCC.

Now suppose that, *ceteris paribus*, five of the 14 voters whose preference ordering is $b \succ c \succ a$ (who are not very happy with the prospect that *a* may be elected) change it to $a \succ b \succ c$ thereby *increasing* *a*'s support. As a result of this change *b* (rather than *c*) will be eliminated in the first round, and *c* (the Condorcet Winner) will beat *a* in the second round—thereby demonstrating the vulnerability of the Plurality with Runoff procedure to non-monotonicity. Notice the other bizarre effect of the preference change of the five voters: the candidate whom they now rank last in their preferences becomes the winner even though it wasn't one before the change.

4.2.2 Absolute Majority Winner Paradox

The Plurality with Runoff procedure is not vulnerable to this paradox because, by definition, if there exists an alternative which is supported by an absolute majority of the voters then this alternative is elected under the Plurality with Runoff procedure.

4.2.3 *Condorcet Loser and Absolute Majority Paradoxes*

Under the Plurality with Runoff procedure an alternative which is a Condorcet Loser or an Absolute Majority Loser may receive the plurality (but not the majority) of votes in the first round, and thus be one of the two alternatives which may compete in the second stage. However, it cannot win in the second stage because, by definition, the majority of voters will prefer the other alternative.

4.2.4 *Pareto-Dominated Candidate Paradox*

The Plurality with Runoff procedure cannot elect a Pareto-dominated alternative, because if all voters prefer alternative w to alternative z then alternative z cannot constitute the top preference of any voter and therefore cannot obtain any votes in any stage of the Plurality with Runoff procedure.

4.2.5 *Truncation Paradox*

This paradox is irrelevant to the Plurality with Runoff procedure in its first version in which voters may go once or twice to the balloting box—voting for just one candidate in each of these times without ranking the candidates.

The Plurality with Runoff procedure in its second version is also not vulnerable to this paradox. To understand why this is so suppose that x and y are the two alternatives which received more votes than each of the remaining alternatives in the first count, and that a voter who prefers x to y contemplates whether it would be worthwhile for him/her to truncate from his/her preference ordering x, y or both. Since there are no more than two counting rounds, the potential truncating voter realizes that s/he cannot change the second-round contestants by truncating any of the candidates whom s/he does not list first in his/her preference ordering. Since s/he prefers x to y, s/he can by truncating x only make x's chances worse or at best maintain its status. To wit, if the truncation involves both x and y, s/he might actually bring about the victory of y (his/her less preferred alternative). If s/he truncates y (and some other alternatives, but not x), s/he does not change the second round outcome. The same is of course true if s/he truncates other alternatives but not x and y. So, the occurrence of the Truncation Paradox is not possible.

4.2.6 *Reinforcement Paradox*

Example 4.2.6.1 demonstrates the vulnerability of the Plurality with Runoff procedure to the Reinforcement Paradox.

4.2.6.1 Example

Suppose there are two districts, I and II. In district I there are 17 voters whose preference orderings among three candidates, *a, b*, and *c*, are as follows:

No. of voters	Preference orderings
4	$a \succ b \succ c$
1	$b \succ a \succ c$
5	$b \succ c \succ a$
6	$c \succ a \succ b$
1	$c \succ b \succ a$

and in district II there are 15 voters whose preference orderings among the three candidates are as follows:

No. of voters	Preference orderings
6	$a \succ c \succ b$
8	$b \succ c \succ a$
1	$c \succ a \succ b$

If all voters vote sincerely then no candidate is ranked first by an absolute majority of the voters in district I. Consequently candidate *a* is deleted from the race after the first round and candidate *b* beats candidate *c* in this district in the second round.

In district II candidate *b*, who is ranked first by an absolute majority of voters, is elected in the first round.

However if, *ceteris paribus*, the two districts are amalgamated into a single district, we obtain the following distribution of preference orderings of the 32 voters:

No. of voters	Preference orderings
4	$a \succ b \succ c$
6	$a \succ c \succ b$
1	$b \succ a \succ c$
13	$b \succ c \succ a$
7	$c \succ a \succ b$
1	$c \succ b \succ a$

If all voters vote sincerely then no candidate is ranked first by an absolute majority of the voters. Consequently c is deleted after the first round and a beats b and is elected in the second round—thus demonstrating the susceptibility of the Plurality with Runoff procedure to the Reinforcement Paradox.

4.2.7 *No Show and Twin Paradoxes*

Example 4.2.7.1 demonstrates the vulnerability of the Plurality with Runoff procedure to the No-Show and to the Twin Paradoxes.

4.2.7.1 Example

Suppose there are 11 voters whose preference orderings among three candidates, a, b, and c, are as follows:

No. of voters	Preference orderings
4	$a \succ b \succ c$
3	$b \succ c \succ a$
1	$c \succ a \succ b$
3	$c \succ b \succ a$

If all voters vote sincerely then no candidate is ranked first by an absolute majority of the voters. Consequently b is deleted after the first round and c beats a in the second round and is elected. Since the election of c is the worst outcome for the voters whose preference ordering is $a \succ b \succ c$, suppose that, *ceteris paribus*, two of them decide not to participate in the election (No-Show). We thus obtain the following distribution of preference orderings:

No. of voters	Preference orderings
2	$a \succ b \succ c$
3	$b \succ c \succ a$
1	$c \succ a \succ b$
3	$c \succ b \succ a$

Here a (rather than b) is eliminated in the first round, and b beats c in the second round. Thus the $a \succ b \succ c$ voters obtained, *ceteris paribus*, a better outcome when two of them did not participate in the election than when all of them participated in the election thereby demonstrating the vulnerability of the Plurality with Runoff procedure to the No-Show Paradox.

This example demonstrates also the vulnerability of the Plurality with Runoff procedure to the of the Twin Paradox. Suppose that, *ceteris paribus*, there are originally only two voters with preference ordering $a \succ b \succ c$. One would expect these voters to welcome other "twin" voters having identical preference ordering to theirs thereby presumably giving an increased weight to their common preference ordering. Yet as we saw, the addition of these twins to the electorate results in the election of c, their worst preference—thereby demonstrating the vulnerability of the Plurality with Runoff procedure to the Twin Paradox.

4.2.8 *Preference Inversion Paradox*

Example 4.2.8.1 demonstrates the vulnerability of the Plurality with Runoff procedure to the Preference Inversion Paradox.

4.2.8.1 Example

Suppose there are 11 voters whose preference orderings among three candidates, a, b, and c, are as follows:

No. of voters	Preference orderings
5	$a \succ b \succ c$
4	$b \succ c \succ a$
2	$c \succ a \succ b$

If all voters vote sincerely for their top preference in the first round, then c will be eliminated at the end of the first round and thereafter a will beat b in the second round. However, if all voters invert their preference orderings then b will be eliminated at the end of the first round and a will beat c in the second round—thus demonstrating the vulnerability of the Plurality with Runoff procedure to the Preference Inversion Paradox.

4.3 The (In)Vulnerability of the Approval Voting Procedure to Various Paradoxes

4.3.1 *The Condorcet Winner Paradox*

Example 4.3.1.1 demonstrates the vulnerability of the Approval Voting procedure to the Condorcet Winner Paradox.

4.3.1.1 Example

This example is adapted from Felsenthal and Maoz (1988, p. 123, Example 2). Suppose there are 49 voters whose preference orderings among three candidates, *a*, *b*, and *c*, are as follows:

No. of voters	Preference orderings
18	$(a) \succ b \succ c$
6	$(b \succ c) \succ a$
8	$(b \succ a) \succ c$
2	$(c \succ a) \succ b$
15	$(c) \succ b \succ a$

The social preference ordering is $b \succ a \succ c$, i.e., *b* is the Condorcet Winner. However, if all voters approve (and vote for) the candidates denoted between parentheses then *a* would get the largest number of approval votes (28) and will thus be elected.

4.3.2 *Absolute Majority Winner Paradox*

Example 4.3.2.1 demonstrates the vulnerability of the Approval Voting procedure to the Absolute Majority Winner Paradox.

4.3.2.1 Example

Suppose there are 100 voters whose preference orderings among three candidates, *a*, *b*, and *c*, are as follows:

No. of voters	Preference orderings
99	$a \succ b \succ c$
1	$b \succ c \succ a$

The social preference ordering is $a \succ b \succ c$, i.e., *a* is the Condorcet Winner who is ranked first by an absolute majority of the voters. However, if only one candidate must be elected and if each voter approves (and votes for) his/her top two preferences, then *b* will be elected despite the fact that *a* is ranked first by an absolute majority of the voters.

4.3.3 *Condorcet Loser, Absolute Majority Loser, and Preference Inversion Paradoxes*

Example 4.3.3.1 demonstrates the vulnerability of the Approval Voting procedure to the Absolute Majority Loser and to the Condorcet Loser Paradoxes.

4.3.3.1 Example

Suppose there are 15 voters whose preference orderings among three candidates, *a*, *b*, and *c*, are as follows:

No. of voters	Preference orderings
6	$(a) \succ b \succ c$
4	$(b) \succ c \succ a$
1	$(c \succ a) \succ b$
4	$(c) \succ b \succ a$

The social preference ordering is $b \succ c \succ a$, i.e., *a* is not only the Condorcet Loser but also the Absolute Majority Loser because this candidate is ranked last by an absolute majority of the voters. However, if only one candidate must be elected and if all voters approve (and vote for) the candidate(s) denoted between parentheses then *a* will be elected.

This example can also be used to demonstrate the susceptibility of the Approval Voting procedure to the Preference Inversion Paradox. If in the above example all voters invert their preference ordering and decide to vote, as before, i.e., either only for their top preference or for their top two preferences, then we obtain the following distribution of votes:

No. of voters	Preference orderings
6	$(c) \succ b \succ a$
4	$(a) \succ c \succ b$
1	$(b \succ a) \succ c$
4	$(a) \succ b \succ c$

Here *a* is not only the Condorcet Winner but also the Absolute Majority Winner and is elected—thereby demonstrating the susceptibility of Approval Voting to the Preference Inversion Paradox.

4.3.4 *The Pareto-Dominated Candidate Paradox*

Example 4.3.4.1 demonstrates the vulnerability of the Approval Voting procedure to the Pareto-Dominated Candidate Paradox.

4.3.4.1 Example

Suppose there are three voters whose preference orderings among three candidates, a, b and c, are as follows:

No. of voters	Preference orderings
2	$a \succ b \succ c$
1	$c \succ a \succ b$

The social preference ordering is $a \succ b \succ c$, i.e., a is the Condorcet Winner. However, if the first two voters with identical preferences approve (and vote for) their top two preferences, while the third voter approves (and votes for) only his/her top ranked candidate, then a tie would occur between the number of votes (2) obtained by candidates a and b, and if this tie were to be broken randomly then there is a 0.5 probability that b would be elected. So if b were to be elected it would demonstrate not only that the Condorcet Winner (a) was not elected but also that a Pareto-dominated candidate can be elected under the Approval Voting procedure. (Note that *all* voters prefer a to b).

4.3.5 Lack of Monotonicity Paradox

The Approval Voting procedure is not vulnerable to lack of monotonicity for the same reasons that the Plurality Voting procedure is not vulnerable to this paradox assuming that the improvement of a candidate's position does not change its approvability status, i.e., the candidates approved of initially will remain approved after the improvement and the same holds for disapproved candidates.

4.3.6 Reinforcement Paradox

The Approval Voting procedure is not vulnerable to the Reinforcement Paradox for the same reasons that the Plurality Voting procedure is not vulnerable to this paradox assuming that the improvement of a candidate's position does not change its approvability status, i.e., the candidates approved of initially will remain approved after the improvement and the same holds for disapproved candidates.

4.3.7 No-Show Paradox

The Approval Voting procedure is not vulnerable to the No-Show Paradox for the same reasons that the Plurality Voting procedure is not vulnerable to this paradox assuming that the improvement of a candidate's position does not change its approvability status, i.e., the candidates approved of initially will remain approved after the improvement and the same holds for disapproved candidates.

4.3.8 *Twin Paradox*

The Approval Voting procedure is not vulnerable to the Twin Paradox for the same reasons that the Plurality Voting procedure is not vulnerable to this paradox assuming that the improvement of a candidate's position does not change its approvability status, i.e., the candidates approved of initially will remain approved after the improvement and the same holds for disapproved candidates.

4.3.9 *Truncation Paradox*

Example 4.3.9.1 demonstrates the vulnerability of the Approval Voting procedure to the Truncation Paradox.

4.3.9.1 Example

Suppose there are 100 voters whose preference orderings among three candidates, *a*, *b*, and *c*, are as follows:

No. of voters	Preference orderings
99	$(a \succ b) \succ c$
1	$(b) \succ a \succ c$

If all voters approve and vote for the candidates listed between parentheses then *b* will be elected. However, by truncating their ballots to include only *a*, the 99 voters (or any proper subset of them consisting of at least 2 voters) will get their most favorite candidate elected thus demonstrating the vulnerability of the Approval Voting procedure to the Truncation Paradox.

4.3.10 *Remark*

Note that under Approval Voting voters may benefit not only by curtailing their ballots of some of the candidates they approve, but also by adding to their ballots some of the candidates whom they disapprove. To see this consider again the first part of Example 4.3.3.1. In this example a was elected. But since a constitutes the last preference of the group of 4 voters who approved and voted only for b, as well as of the group of 4 voters who approved and voted for only for c, any of these groups would be better off if, *ceteris paribus*, they would vote also for their second-ranked (disapproved) candidate.

4.3.11 The SCC Paradox

The Approval Voting procedure satisfies SCC if voters are assumed to approve and vote for precisely the same available candidates in all subsets of the candidates. This conclusion follows from the fact that the approval tallies of the candidates remain the same in all subsets. Hence the winners remain winners in all subsets they are members of.[1]

4.4 The (In)Vulnerability of the Successive Elimination Procedure to Various Paradoxes

4.4.1 Absolute Majority Winner and Condorcet Winner Paradoxes

If voters are assumed to vote sincerely in each voting round then it follows that a Condorcet Winner—and *a fortiori* an Absolute Majority Winner—will always be elected under the Successive Elimination procedure because these alternatives will always beat any other alternative pitted against them in any voting round in which they are first included through the last voting round.

4.4.2 Absolute Majority Loser and Condorcet Loser Paradoxes

If voters are assumed to vote sincerely in each voting round then it follows that a Condorcet Loser—and *a fortiori* an Absolute Majority Loser—cannot be elected

---

[1]However, it may be rational sometime, under the Approval Voting procedure too, to vote for previously unapproved candidate(s) rather than to keep voting only for previously approved candidate(s) or abstain when some previously approved (and losing) candidate(s) is (are) no longer available. Thus, for example, it would be beneficial for the 15 $(c) \succ b \succ a$ voters in Example 4.3.1.1 to vote for their previously unapproved candidate (b)—and thereby obtain, *ceteris paribus*, the election of b, than to abstain and obtain the election of a. In such eventualities the Approval Voting procedure too may be considered as being vulnerable to the SCC Paradox.

under the Successive Elimination procedure because these alternatives will always be beaten by every other alternative pitted against them in any voting round in which they are first included through the last voting round.

4.4.3 Pareto-Dominated Candidate, SCC, No-Show, and Dependence on Order of Voting (DOV) Paradoxes

Example 4.4.3.1 demonstrates the vulnerability of the Successive Elimination procedure to the election of a Pareto-dominated candidate. A necessary condition for this to happen is that the social preference ordering is cyclical and there are at least four candidates (Fishburn 1982, p. 131).

4.4.3.1 Example

Suppose there are 11 voters whose preference orderings among four candidates, *a*, *b*, *c*, and *d*, are as follows:

No. of voters	Preference orderings
3	$a \succ b \succ c \succ d$
2	$c \succ a \succ b \succ d$
1	$c \succ d \succ a \succ b$
5	$d \succ a \succ b \succ c$

Thus the social preference ordering is cyclical ($b \succ c \succ d \succ a \succ b$). Suppose further that all the voters always vote sincerely for their preferred candidate in each round, and that the order in which the divisions are carried out is as follows:

In round 1: *d* against *a*;
In round 2: the winner of round 1 against *c*;
In round 3: the winner of round 2 against *b*;

Given this order *d* beats *a* (6:5) in the first round, *c* beats *d* (6:5) in the second round, and *b* beats *c* (8:3) in the third round and becomes the ultimate winner. Note, however, that *b* is a Pareto-dominated candidate because *all* the voters prefer *a* to *b*.

This example can also be used to demonstrate the vulnerability of the Successive Elimination procedure to SCC.

If, *ceteris paribus*, *d* is deleted, then in the first round *a* will beat *c* (8:3), and in the second round *a* will beat *b* (11:0) and thus *a* will become the ultimate winner—in violation of SCC.

Similarly, this example can also be used to demonstrate the vulnerability of the Successive Elimination procedure to the No-Show Paradox.

If *ceteris paribus*, two of the voters whose top preference is d decide not to participate, then a becomes the Condorcet Winner and hence will be elected under the Successive Elimination procedure. Note that this outcome is preferred over the election of b by the two $d \succ a \succ b \succ c$ voters who decided not to participate—thus demonstrating the vulnerability of the Successive Elimination procedure to the No-Show Paradox.

This example can also be used to demonstrate the vulnerability of the Successive Elimination procedure to the order in which the alternatives are voted upon (Dependence on Order of Voting Paradox) when the social preference ordering is cyclical.

Given the above preference orderings of the 11 voters, if the order of the divisions in each round were changed such that:

In round 1: a against b;
In round 2: the winner of round 1 against c;
In round 3: the winner of round 2 against d;
Then in the first round a would beat b (11:0), in the second round a would also beat c (8:3), but in the third round d would beat a (6:5) and become the ultimate winner.

4.4.4 Lack of Monotonicity Paradox

Assuming that voters vote sincerely in each voting round and that the order in which the alternatives are voted upon stays the same, it follows that the Successive Elimination procedure is invulnerable to monotonicity failure in *fixed electorates*. This is so because if alternative x is the ultimate winner when the number of voters is fixed then x will *a fortiori* continue to be the winner if some voters who previously voted against x will change their minds and vote for x. However, the Successive Elimination procedure may be susceptible to lack of monotonicity in *variable electorates*. For examples of such monotonicity failure see Felsenthal and Nurmi (2016, 2017).

4.4.5 Reinforcement Paradox

Example 4.4.5.1 demonstrates the vulnerability of the Successive Elimination procedure to the Reinforcement Paradox.

4.4.5.1 Example

Suppose there are two districts, I and II. In district I there are three voters whose preference orderings among four candidates are as follows:

No. of voters	Preference orderings
1	$a \succ b \succ d \succ c$
1	$b \succ d \succ c \succ a$
1	$d \succ c \succ a \succ b$

and in district II there are four voters whose preference orderings among the four candidates are as follows:

No. of voters	Preference orderings
3	$c \succ d \succ b \succ a$
1	$d \succ a \succ b \succ c$

If the order of divisions in each district is:

b versus *d* in round 1;
winner of 1st round against *a* in round 2;
winner of 2nd round against *c* in round 3;

then in each district *c* will be the ultimate winner.
However if, *ceteris paribus*, the two districts are amalgamated into a single district of seven voters, then *d* becomes the Condorcet Winner and will therefore be elected under the Successive Elimination procedure—in violation of the Reinforcement postulate.

4.4.6 Twin Paradox

Example 4.4.6.1 demonstrates the vulnerability of the Successive Elimination procedure to the Twin Paradox.

4.4.6.1 Example

This example is due to Moulin (1988, p. 54). Suppose there are six voters whose preference orderings among three candidates, *a*, *b*, and *c*, are as follows:

No. of voters	Preference orderings
2	$a \succ b \succ c$
2	$b \succ c \succ a$
1	$c \succ a \succ b$
1	$c \succ b \succ a$

Suppose further that the order in which the divisions are conducted is as follows:

a versus b in round 1; winner of round 1 versus c in round 2; and that if there is a tie between two candidates in any of the divisions it is broken lexicographically, i.e., in favor of the candidate who is denoted by the letter that is closer to the beginning of the alphabet.

Accordingly, there is a tie between a and b in the first round which is broken in favor of a, and in the second round c beats a and becomes the ultimate winner.

In view of this result one could expect that, *ceteris paribus*, the single $c \succ b \succ a$ voter should welcome if an additional "twin" voter would join the electorate thereby providing more weight to their common preferences. However, an addition of a second $c \succ b \succ a$ voter would result, *ceteris paribus*, in a net loss to the first $c \succ b \succ a$ voter because b would become the Condorcet Winner and hence also the ultimate winner under the Successive Elimination procedure—thus demonstrating the vulnerability of the Successive Elimination procedure to the Twin Paradox.

4.4.7 Truncation Paradox

Example 4.4.7.1 demonstrates the vulnerability of the Successive Elimination procedure to the Truncation Paradox.

4.4.7.1 Example

Suppose there are six voters with the following preference orderings:

No. of voters	Preference orderings
1	$a \succ b \succ c \succ d$
1	$c \succ b \succ a \succ d$
2	$c \succ d \succ b \succ a$
2	$d \succ a \succ b \succ c$

Suppose further that the order in which the divisions are conducted is as follows:

First round: b versus c;
Second round: winner of 1st round versus d;
Third round: winner of 2nd round versus a;

Additionally, suppose that if a tie occurs between two candidates it is broken in favor of the one denoted by a letter closer to the beginning of the alphabet.

Accordingly, in the first round there is a tie between b and c which is broken in favor of b. In the second round d beats b, and in the third round d beats a and hence becomes the ultimate winner. This is of course a very bad outcome for the single voter whose preference ordering is $a \succ b \succ c \succ d$. So suppose that, *ceteris paribus*, this voter would truncate his/her preferences between *b, c,* and *d*, and indicate just his/her top preference, *a*, i.e., this voter will participate only in the third round in which *a* will compete against the winner from the second round. As a result of such truncation *c* would beat *b* in the first round, *c* would beat also *d* in the second round, but in the third round there would be a tie between *a* and *c*—which will be broken in favor of *a*, a much better result for the $a \succ b \succ c \succ d$ voter, thus demonstrating the vulnerability of the Successive Elimination procedure to the Truncation Paradox.

4.4.8 *Preference Inversion Paradox*

Example 4.4.8.1 demonstrates the vulnerability of Successive Elimination procedure to the Preference Inversion Paradox.

4.4.8.1 Example

Suppose that nine voters have to elect one out of three candidates, *a*, *b*, or *c*, under the Successive Elimination procedure and that their preference orderings among these candidates are as follows:

No. of voters	Preference orderings
4	$a \succ b \succ c$
3	$b \succ c \succ a$
2	$c \succ a \succ b$

Suppose further that the order of voting is as follows:

First round: *a* versus *b;*
Second round: winner of 1st round versus *c*.

Accordingly, in the first round *a* will beat *b*, and in the second round *c* will beat *a* and will become the ultimate winner. *Ceteris paribus*, *c* will also be elected if each of the three voters inverts his/her preference ordering.

A summary of the performance of the above four non-ranked systems with respect to the 13 paradoxes is presented in Table 4.1.

Table 4.1 (In)Vulnerability of non-ranked voting procedures to 13 voting paradoxes

Paradox	Procedure			
	Plurality	Plurality with Runoff	Approval Voting	Successive Elimination
Condorcet Winner Paradox	+	+	+	–
Absolute Majority Winner Paradox	–	–	⊕	–
Condorcet Loser Paradox	⊕	–	⊕	–
Absolute Majority Loser Paradox	⊕	–	⊕	–
Pareto Dominated Candidate	–	–	⊕	⊕
Lack of Monotonicity	–	⊕	–	–
Reinforcement	–	+	–	+
No-Show	–	+	–	+
Twin	–	+	–	+
Truncation	–	–	+	+
Subset Choice Condition (SCC)	+	+	–	+
Preference Inversion	+	+	+	+
Dependence on Order of Voting (DOV)	–	–	–	+
Total ⊕ signs	2	1	4	1
Total +& ⊕ signs	5	7	7	8

Notes

A + sign indicates that a procedure is vulnerable to the specified paradox;

A ⊕ sign indicates that a procedure is vulnerable to the specified paradox which seems to us an especially intolerable paradox;

A – sign indicates that a procedure is invulnerable to the specified paradox;

It is assumed that all voters have linear preference orderings among all competing candidates.

Exercises

Problem 4.1 Consider the following 11-voter, 3-alternative profile.

No. of voters	Preference orderings
5	$a \succ c \succ b$
4	$b \succ c \succ a$
2	$c \succ b \succ a$

Determine (i) the Plurality Voting winner; (ii) the Plurality with Runoff winner, (iii) the Condorcet Winner if one exists, (iv) the Approval Voting winner if the last 2 voters approve of (and vote for) their top two preferences whereas the remaining nine voters approve of (and vote for) only their top preference, and (v) the winner under the Successive Elimination procedure regardless of the order in which the alternatives are voted upon.

Problem 4.2 Construct a preference profile over 4 alternatives so that there is no Condorcet Winner.

Problem 4.3 Construct a 3-alternative, 5-voter example where the Plurality with Runoff procedure fails to elect the Condorcet Winner.

Problem 4.4 Construct a 3-alternative profile where the Plurality Voting procedure, Plurality with Runoff procedure and the Borda count each result in a different choice.

Problem 4.5 Consider the following profile containing all six possible strict rankings (no ties) over three alternatives *a, b, c*.

No. of voters	Preference orderings
$v(1)$	$a \succ b \succ c$
$v(2)$	$a \succ c \succ b$
$v(3)$	$b \succ a \succ c$
$v(4)$	$b \succ c \succ a$
$v(5)$	$c \succ a \succ b$
$v(6)$	$c \succ b \succ a$

For any profile of strict preferences $v(j)$, $j = 1, \ldots, 6$ denotes the number of individuals having the j'th ranking. Express in terms of values of $v(j)$ a sufficient condition for c being the unanimity winner, i.e., ranked first by all individuals.

Express in terms of inequalities those profiles where a is the Plurality Voting winner.

Express in terms of inequalities those profiles where a is the Condorcet Winner. When would alternative c be unanimously elected?

Answers to Exercises

Problem 4.1 The Plurality Voting winner is a; the Plurality with Runoff winner is b; the Condorcet Winner is c; the Approval Voting winner is b; the Successive Elimination winner is c (the Condorcet Winner).

Problem 4.2 A 4-alternative profile where there is no Condorcet Winner is, for example, the following profile:

No. of voters	Preference orderings
5	$a \succ c \succ b \succ d$
4	$b \succ d \succ a \succ c$
2	$c \succ d \succ a \succ b$

Here the social preference ordering is cyclical ($b \succ d \succ a \succ c \succ b$).

Problem 4.3 Here is an example:

No. of voters	Preference orderings
2	$a \succ c \succ b$
2	$b \succ c \succ a$
1	$c \succ b \succ a$

Here c is the Condorcet Winner but will be eliminated at the end of the first counting round and then b will beat a in the second round to become the ultimate winner.

Problem 4.4 Here is an example:

No. of voters	Preference orderings
5	$a \succ c \succ b$
4	$b \succ c \succ a$
2	$c \succ b \succ a$

Here a is the Plurality Voting winner, b is the winner in the Plurality with Runoff procedure, and c is the Borda winner.

Problem 4.5 Alternative a is the Plurality Voting winner if $v(1) + v(2) > v(3) + v(4)$ and $v(1) + v(2) > v(5) + v(6)$.

Alternative a is the Condorcet Winner if $v(1) + v(2) + v(5) > v(3) + v(4) + v(6)$ and $v(1) + v(2) + v(3) > v(4) + v(5) + v(6)$.

Alternative c is the unanimity winner if $v(5) + v(6)$ equals the total number of voters.

References

Felsenthal, D. S. (2012). Review of paradoxes afflicting procedures for electing a single candidate. In D. S. Felsenthal & M. Machover (Eds.), *Electoral systems: Paradoxes, assumptions, and procedures* (pp. 19–92). Berlin: Springer (Ch. 3).

Felsenthal, D. S., & Maoz, Z. (1988). A comparative analysis of sincere and sophisticated voting under the plurality and approval procedures. *Behavioral Science, 33,* 116–130.

Felsenthal, D. S., & Nurmi, H. (2016). Two types of participation failure under nine voting methods in variable electorates. *Public Choice, 168,* 115–135.

Felsenthal, D. S., & Nurmi, H. (2017). *Monotonicity failures afflicting procedures for electing a single candidate*. Cham, Switzerland: Springer.

Fishburn, P. C. (1982). Monotonicity paradoxes in the theory of elections. *Discrete Applied Mathematics, 4,* 119–134.

Moulin, H. (1988). Condorcet's principle implies the No-Show paradox. *Journal of Economic Theory, 45,* 53–64.

Chapter 5
The (In)Vulnerability of Ranked Voting Procedures that Are Not Condorcet–Consistent to Various Paradoxes

Abstract The (in)vulnerability of six ranked voting procedures which are not Condorcet–consistent (Borda count, Alternative vote, Coombs' procedure, Bucklin's procedure, Range Voting and Majority Judgment) to 13 paradoxes is examined in this chapter. For those systems that are vulnerable to some voting paradoxes the vulnerability is demonstrated through illustrative examples showing that there are profiles where the paradoxes in question happen when the respective procedures are in use. And for those systems that are invulnerable to some voting paradoxes the invulnerability is explained.

Keywords Condorcet–consistent procedures · Ranked voting procedures · (In)vulnerability to voting paradoxes

5.1 The (In)Vulnerability of Borda's Procedure to Various Paradoxes

5.1.1 The Condorcet Winner and the Absolute Majority Winner Paradoxes

Example 5.1.1.1 demonstrates simultaneously the vulnerability of Borda's procedure to the Absolute Majority Winner Paradox (and thus also to the Condorcet Winner Paradox).

This chapter is partly based on Felsenthal (2012) which contains several examples devised by the second–named author.

All ranked procedures that are not Condorcet–consistent violate Smith's (1973) Condorcet Principle (cf. Sect. 2.1.3 in Chap. 2). As is demonstrated in Example 6.5.11.1 (in Chap. 6) some of the Condorcet–consistent procedures too may violate this Principle.

All the procedures surveyed in this chapter are invulnerable to the Dependence on Order of Voting (DOV) Paradox (cf. Sect. 2.2.8 in Chap. 2) because under these procedures all candidates are voted upon simultaneously rather than sequentially.

D. S. Felsenthal and H. Nurmi, *Voting Procedures for Electing a Single Candidate*, SpringerBriefs in Economics, https://doi.org/10.1007/978-3-319-74033-1_5

5.1.1.1 Example

Suppose there are 100 voters who have to elect one out of three candidates, *a*, *b*, *c*, under Borda's procedure, and whose preference orderings are as follows:

No. of voters	Preference orderings
66	$a \succ b \succ c$
33	$b \succ c \succ a$
1	$c \succ b \succ a$

The number of Borda points awarded to candidates *a*, *b*, and *c*, are 132, 133, and 35, respectively, so candidate *b* is elected. However, note that candidate *a* is not only the Condorcet Winner but also an Absolute Majority Winner because an absolute majority of the voters rank candidate *a* as their top preference.

5.1.2 Condorcet Loser Paradox

An alternative, *x*, is a Condorcet Loser, if the majority of voters prefer every other alternative to *x*. In this case the sum of entries in row *x* of the pairwise comparison matrix is no larger than $(v - 1)(n - 1)/2$. (Here *v* denotes the number of voters and *n* the number of candidates.)[1] This cannot be the maximal row sum in any pairwise comparison matrix since the grand total sum of all row sums would in that case be at most $n(v - 1)(n - 1)/2$, i.e., strictly smaller than the total of Borda scores of all candidates as stated in Sect. 3.2.1 (cf. Chap. 3) above. Hence, at least one alternative has to have a strictly larger Borda score than the Condorcet Loser *x*. Therefore a Condorcet Loser cannot be elected by the Borda count.

5.1.3 Absolute Majority Loser Paradox

This is a special case of the Condorcet Loser Paradox. An alternative, *x*, is an Absolute Majority Loser if it is ranked last by an absolute majority of the voters. Because Borda's procedure is invulnerable to the Condorcet Loser Paradox it is, *a fortiori*, invulnerable to the Absolute Majority Loser Paradox.

[1]A pairwise comparison matrix is a matrix with *n* rows and *n* columns (where *n* is the number of candidates). In such a matrix the entry in row *x* and column *y* denotes the number of voters who rank candidate *x* ahead of candidate *y* in their preference ordering and the entry in row *y* and column *x* is the complementary number denoting the number of voters who rank candidate *y* ahead of candidate *x*. The cells along the main diagonal of this matrix are left empty.

5.1.4 *Pareto-Dominated Candidate Paradox*

An alternative, x, is Pareto-dominated if *all* voters prefer some other alternative, say y, to x. So if y Pareto dominates x, it follows that x receives a strictly smaller number of points than y from every voter. Therefore, x's Borda score is strictly smaller than y's and the former cannot be elected under Borda's procedure.

5.1.5 *Lack of Monotonicity Paradox*

A voting procedure may suffer from lack of monotonicity if, *ceteris paribus*:

(i) A winning alternative, x, may become a loser if some voters who previously ranked x lower in their preference ordering now rank x higher in their preference ordering, or
(ii) A winning alternative, x, may become a loser if some additional voters join the electorate who rank x at the top of their preference ordering, or
(iii) A losing alternative, z, may become a winner if some voters who previously ranked z at some specified spot in their preference ordering now rank z in a lower spot in their preference ordering, or
(iv) A losing alternative, z, may become a winner if some new voters join the electorate who rank z at the bottom of their preference ordering.

Borda's procedure is not vulnerable to any type of the afore–mentioned monotonicity failures for a simple reason: if a candidate, x, is elected by a given electorate—which implies that this candidate obtained the largest number of Borda points—then this candidate will surely be re–elected if, *ceteris paribus*, any of the voters who originally ranked x lower in their preference orderings will change their minds and rank x higher in their preference orderings, or if, *ceteris paribus*, additional voters join the electorate who will rank x at the top of their preference orderings. This is due to the fact that such an improvement in x's position gives it a strictly larger Borda score than before the improvement. At the same time, no other candidate receives a higher Borda score as a result of the improvement of x's position.

Similarly, if x was not originally the winner then the fact that, *ceteris paribus*, some voters lowered x in their preference orderings or that additional voters joined the electorate whose bottom preference is x cannot increase the number of points obtained by x—thereby x must remain a non–winner.

5.1.6 *Reinforcement Paradox*

Borda's procedure is invulnerable to this paradox. This is so because the joint electorate can be represented by a pairwise comparison matrix where each of its

i, j cells represents the sum of the i, j cells in the separate electorates—so if x was the row with the largest sum in each of the several pairwise comparison matrices it must also be the row with the largest sum in the joint pairwise comparison matrix.

5.1.7 No–Show Paradox

The Borda procedure is not susceptible to the No–Show Paradox because the winning alternative under Borda's procedure is the alternative whose sum in the pairwise comparison matrix is largest. Therefore any single voter who abstains decreases by 1 the entries in the pairwise comparison matrix that fit his/her preference ordering. Thus, for example, if there are four alternatives, a, b, c, d, and, *ceteris paribus*, a voter whose preference ordering is $a \succ b \succ c \succ d$ abstains, then the entries in the cells a,b, a,c, a,d, b,c, b,d, and c,d decrease by 1—consequently the sum in row a (the most preferred alternative) is decreased by 3, the sum in row b (the second most preferred alternative) is decreased by 2, the sum in row c (the third most preferred alternative) is decreased by 1, and the sum of row d (the least preferred alternative) is not changed. So a voter whose preference ordering is $a \succ b \succ c \succ d$ not only cannot benefit by abstaining but may obtain a worse outcome by doing so as there is an increasing probability that the less preferable an alternative is the more likely it may end up as the selected alternative because the decrease in the sum of its row becomes increasingly smaller: the sum of his/her top alternative (a) is decreased by 3, the sum of his/her second alternative (b) is decreased by 2, the sum of his/her third alternative (c) is decreased by 1, and the sum of his/her least preferred alternative (d) does not change.

5.1.8 Twin Paradox

As the Borda procedure is not susceptible to the No–Show Paradox it is also not susceptible to the Twin Paradox. This is so because if the Borda procedure selects an alternative, x, when only one voter has the preference ordering $x \succ y \succ z$ it implies that row x in the pairwise comparison matrix has the largest sum. Therefore, *ceteris paribus*, this procedure will select x *a fortiori* if another voter with the same preference ordering joins the electorate or another voter changes his/her preference ordering to $x \succ y \succ z$, thereby increasing further the sum of row x in the pairwise comparison matrix.

5.1.9 Truncation and SCC Paradoxes

Example 5.1.9.1 demonstrates the vulnerability of Borda's procedure to the Truncation Paradox.

5.1.9.1 Example

Suppose that seven voters have to elect one out of four candidates *a*–*d* under Borda's procedure, and that their preference orderings among the candidates are as follows:

No. of voters	Preference orderings
3	$a \succ b \succ c \succ d$
1	$b \succ c \succ a \succ d$
1	$b \succ c \succ d \succ a$
2	$c \succ d \succ a \succ b$

Here the Borda scores of *a*, *b*, *c*, and *d* are 12, 12, 13, and 5, respectively, so *c* is the winner.

Now suppose that, *ceteris paribus*, the three voters with preference ordering $a \succ b \succ c \succ d$ (who are not happy with the prospect that *c* will be elected) decide to truncate candidate *c* from their ballots. In this case we apply the Borda Truncated scoring system proposed by Fishburn (1974, p. 543) for truncated ballots. According to this system when there are *k* candidates of whom some voter(s) rank in their ballots only $k - t$ candidates ($k > t \geq 1$) and truncate from their ballots the remaining *t* candidates, then each of the truncated candidates gets 0 points from each of the truncated ballots, whereas the first-ranked candidate in each of these ballots gets $k - t$ points, the second-ranked candidate gets $k - t - 1$ points,…, and the last ranked candidate in these truncated ballots gets 1 point. As a result of this (revised) scoring system the Borda scores of *a*, *b*, *c*, *d* in this example are 12, 12, 10, and 8, respectively, so there is a tie between *a* and *b*—which is a preferable outcome for the three truncating voters, thereby demonstrating the vulnerability of Borda's procedure to the Truncation Paradox.

Example 5.1.9.2 demonstrates the vulnerability of Borda's procedure to the SCC Paradox.

5.1.9.2 Example

Suppose that 11 voters have to elect one out of three candidates, *a*, *b*, or *c*, under Borda's procedure and that their preference orderings among these candidates are as follows:

No. of voters	Preference orderings
3	$a \succ c \succ b$
3	$b \succ a \succ c$
5	$c \succ b \succ a$

Accordingly, the number of Borda points awarded (as usual, according to the rule mentioned in Sect. 3.2.1 in Chap. 3) to candidates *a*, *b*, and *c*, are 9, 11, and 13, respectively—so candidate *c* is elected.

Now suppose that, *ceteris paribus*, candidate *b* drops out of the race. In this case the number of Borda points awarded to candidates *a* and *c* are 6 and 5, respectively, so candidate *a* would be elected—in violation of SCC.

5.1.10 Preference Inversion Paradox

The Borda count is invulnerable to the Preference Inversion Paradox since inverting rankings implies inverting the order of the Borda scores of candidates. Arguably a perfectly symmetrical Condorcet Paradox profile where each candidate is placed in each position by equally many voters will result in a tie among all candidates and so does its reversal. However, in this type of profile all anonymous and neutral procedures result in an *n*–way tie (*n* being the number of candidates). Apart from these special profiles, it has been shown that the Borda count is the only positional procedure that is invulnerable to the Preference Inversion Paradox (Saari and Barney 2003).

5.2 The (In)Vulnerability of the Alternative Vote Procedure to Various Paradoxes

5.2.1 Condorcet Winner, Lack of Monotonicity, Reinforcement, No–Show, Twin, Preference Inversion, and SCC Paradoxes

The Alternative Vote procedure is vulnerable to the Condorcet Winner, Lack of Monotonicity, Reinforcement, No–Show, Twin, Preference Inversion, and SCC Paradoxes. The same examples that were used to demonstrate the vulnerability of the Plurality with Runoff procedure to all these paradoxes in Chap. 4 can also be used to demonstrate the vulnerability of the Alternative Vote procedure to these paradoxes.

Specifically, Example 4.2.1.1 can be used to demonstrate the vulnerability of the Alternative Vote procedure to the Condorcet Winner, to lack of monotonicity,[2]

[2]A display of negative responsiveness (or lack of monotonicity) under the Alternative Vote procedure has actually occurred recently in the March 2009 mayoral election in Burlington, Vermont. Among the three biggest vote getters, the Republican got the most first–place votes, the Democrat the fewest, and the Progressive won after the Democrat was eliminated. Yet if many of those who ranked the Republican first had ranked the Progressive first, the Republican would have been eliminated and the Progressive would have lost to the Democrat. In March 2010 Burlington replaced the Alternative Vote procedure for electing its mayor with the Plurality with Runoff procedure—which is also susceptible to negative responsiveness. See detailed report in http://rangevoting.org/Burlington.html

and to the SCC Paradoxes; Example 4.2.6.1 can be used to demonstrate the vulnerability of the Alternative Vote procedure to the Reinforcement Paradox, Example 4.2.7.1 can be used to demonstrate the vulnerability of the Alternative Vote procedure to the No–Show and Twin Paradoxes, and Example 4.2.8.1 can be used to demonstrate the vulnerability of the Alternative Vote procedure to the Preference Inversion Paradox. This is due to the fact that in three–candidate settings the Plurality Runoff and the Alternative Vote procedures are equivalent: if one round only is needed the criterion of winning is the same, and if two rounds are needed, the former qualifies two largest vote–getters thereby eliminating the candidate with the smallest number of first ranks, i.e. precisely as in the Alternative Vote procedure.

5.2.2 *Absolute Majority Winner Paradox*

The Alternative Vote procedure, by definition, always elects a candidate who is ranked first by an absolute majority of the voters. Therefore, it is invulnerable to the Absolute Majority Winner Paradox.

5.2.3 *Absolute Majority Loser, Condorcet Loser, and Pareto-Dominated Candidate Paradoxes*

Since the Alternative Vote procedure seeks, in every counting round, to find a candidate who is ranked first by an absolute majority of the voters, it follows that it cannot elect either a Condorcet Loser, an Absolute Majority Loser, or a Pareto-dominated candidate.

5.2.4 *Truncation Paradox*

Example 5.2.4.1 demonstrates the vulnerability of the Alternative Vote procedure to the Truncation Paradox.

5.2.4.1 Example

Suppose there are 103 voters whose preference orderings among four candidates, a, b, c, and d, are as indicated below and who must elect one of these candidates under the Alternative Vote procedure.

No. of voters	Preference orderings
33	$a \succ b \succ c \succ d$
29	$b \succ a \succ c \succ d$
24	$c \succ b \succ a \succ d$
17	$d \succ c \succ b \succ a$

Since none of the four candidates is ranked first by an absolute majority of the voters, candidate d (who is ranked first by the smallest number of voters) is eliminated. As this does not yet lead to a winner, b is eliminated, whereupon a wins.

Suppose now that, *ceteris paribus*, those 17 voters who rank a last decide to truncate their preference ordering and list only their top preference, d. In this case d will be eliminated first (as before), but since these 17 voters did not indicate their preference ordering among the remaining candidates, candidate c (rather than b) will be eliminated thereafter—whereupon b wins. This result is preferred by these 17 voters to the election of a, thereby demonstrating the vulnerability of the Alternative Vote procedure to the Truncation Paradox.

5.2.5 *Remark*

The UK conducted a referendum in May 2011 regarding whether to replace its Plurality Voting procedure in parliamentary elections with the Alternative Vote procedure. It may therefore be interesting to note that when there are only three competing candidates (as is usually the case in parliamentary elections in England), the Alternative Vote procedure is more Condorcet–efficient, i.e., is more likely to elect the Condorcet Winner when one exists, than the Plurality Voting procedure. This is so because, by definition, a necessary and sufficient condition for a Condorcet Winner (or any other candidate) to be elected under the Plurality Voting procedure is that s/he will constitute the top preference of a plurality of the voters, whereas for a Condorcet Winner to be elected under the Alternative Vote procedure when there are three candidates it is sufficient (but not necessary) that the Condorcet Winner constitutes the top preference of a plurality of the voters. This is so because if there exist three candidates, a, b, and c, such that the social preference ordering is $a \succ b \succ c$ and a constitutes the top preference of the plurality of voters, then either b or c (but not a) must be eliminated in the first counting round, and as a is the Condorcet Winner s/he must necessarily beat the remaining alternative in the second counting round. In other words, in three–candidates races it is more likely that the Condorcet Winner is elected under the Alternative Vote procedure than under Plurality Voting because it is strictly more likely to be ranked first *or* second than to be ranked first in terms of plurality votes.

So while it is a sufficient condition for a Condorcet Winner to be elected under the Alternative Vote procedure when there are three candidates such that the Condorcet Winner constitutes the top preference of a plurality of the voters, it is not a necessary condition because, as can be ascertained from Example 4.1.1.1 (Chap. 4) a Condorcet Winner (b) can be elected under the Alternative Vote procedure when there are three candidates even though it does not constitute the top preference of a plurality of the voters.

However, it is no longer a sufficient condition for a Condorcet Winner who is ranked first by a plurality of the voters to be elected under the Alternative Vote procedure once there are more than three candidates. This is demonstrated in Example 5.2.5.1

5.2.5.1 Example

This example is due partly to Moshé Machover who provided the first–named author general guidance in its construction (private communication 13.12.2010). Suppose there are 85 voters whose preference orderings among four candidates, a, b, c, and d, are as indicated below and who must elect one of these candidates under the Alternative Vote procedure.

No. of voters	Preference orderings
15	$a \succ b \succ c \succ d$
10	$a \succ c \succ b \succ d$
13	$b \succ a \succ c \succ d$
10	$b \succ c \succ a \succ d$
14	$c \succ a \succ b \succ d$
10	$c \succ b \succ a \succ d$
6	$d \succ c \succ a \succ b$
7	$d \succ b \succ a \succ c$

The social preference ordering here is $a \succ b \succ c \succ d$, i.e., candidate a is the Condorcet Winner who is ranked first by a plurality of the voters. However, as none of the candidates is ranked first by an absolute majority of the voters, one deletes first candidate d according to the Alternative Vote procedure, and thereafter one deletes candidate a, whereupon candidate b becomes the winner.

5.3 The (In)Vulnerability of Coombs' Procedure to Various Paradoxes

5.3.1 *Condorcet Winner Paradox*

Example 5.3.1.1 demonstrates the vulnerability of Coombs' procedure to the Condorcet Winner Paradox.

5.3.1.1 Example

This example is due to Nicolaus Tideman (private communication to the first–named author 8.9.2010). Suppose that 45 voters have to elect under Coombs' procedure one out of three candidates, *a*, *b*, or *c*, and that their preference orderings among these three candidates are as follows:

No. of voters	Preference orderings
1	$a \succ b \succ c$
10	$a \succ c \succ b$
11	$b \succ a \succ c$
11	$b \succ c \succ a$
10	$c \succ a \succ b$
2	$c \succ b \succ a$

Here *b* is the Condorcet Winner, but is eliminated first according to Coombs' procedure and thereafter *c* is elected.

5.3.2 *Absolute Majority Winner Paradox*

Coombs' procedure, by definition, always elects a candidate who is ranked first by an absolute majority of the voters.

5.3.3 *Absolute Majority Loser, Condorcet Loser, and Pareto-Dominated Candidate Paradoxes*

Since Coombs' procedure seeks, in every counting round, to find a candidate who is ranked first by an absolute majority of the voters, it follows that it cannot elect either a Condorcet Loser, an Absolute Majority Loser, or a Pareto-dominated candidate.

5.3.4 *Remark*

It is not clear whether Coombs' procedure is more Condorcet–efficient than either the Plurality Voting or the Alternative Vote procedures. As we have already stated in Rem. 5.2.5, a necessary and sufficient condition for a Condorcet Winner to be elected under the Plurality Voting procedure is that the Condorcet Winner constitutes the top preference of a plurality of the voters. This condition is sufficient (but not necessary) for a Condorcet Winner to be elected under the Alternative Vote procedure when there are three candidates. However, as is demonstrated in Example 5.3.1.1 above, this condition is neither necessary nor sufficient for a Condorcet Winner to be elected under Coombs' procedure. On the other hand, as argued by Coombs (1964, p. 399), a sufficient condition for a Condorcet Winner to be elected under his proposed procedure is that the voters' preferences are single–peaked along a single dimension. But under both the Plurality Voting and Alternative Vote procedures a Condorcet Winner may not be elected when the voters' preferences are single–peaked along a single dimension. To see this consider Example 5.3.4.1.

5.3.4.1 Example

Suppose there are 13 voters who must elect one out of three candidates, a, b, or c, and whose preference orderings among these candidates are as follows:

No. of voters	Preference orderings
1	$a \succ b \succ c$
2	$a \succ c \succ b$
4	$b \succ a \succ c$
6	$c \succ a \succ b$

Here a is the Condorcet Winner, the voters' preferences are single–peaked, and a is elected under Coombs' procedure. However, under the Plurality Voting and Alternative Vote procedures c is elected.

5.3.5 *Lack of Monotonicity Paradox*

In Example 5.3.1.1 above candidate c was elected under Coombs' procedure although candidate b is the Condorcet Winner. Now suppose that, *ceteris paribus*, the 11 voters whose preference ordering is $b \succ a \succ c$ (who are not happy with the prospect that c will be elected) are motivated to *increase* c's support by changing their preference ordering to $b \succ c \succ a$. Candidate b is still the Condorcet Winner but as a result of this change a (rather than b) will first be eliminated under Coombs' procedure, and thereafter b will be elected—in violation of the monotonicity postulate.

5.3.6 *No–Show, Truncation, and Preference Inversion Paradoxes*

Example 5.3.6.1 demonstrates the vulnerability of Coombs' procedure to the No–Show, Truncation, and Preference Inversion Paradoxes.

5.3.6.1 Example

Suppose there are 15 voters who must elect one out of three candidates, *a*, *b*, or *c*, under Coombs' procedure, and whose preference orderings among these candidates are as follows:

No. of voters	Preference orderings
4	$a \succ b \succ c$
4	$b \succ c \succ a$
5	$c \succ a \succ b$
2	$c \succ b \succ a$

Here no candidate is ranked first by an absolute majority of the voters. Hence, according to Coombs' procedure, *a* is eliminated in the first round and thereafter *b* is elected.

Now suppose that, *ceteris paribus*, the two voters with preference ordering $c \succ b \succ a$ decide not to participate in the election. In this case *b* is eliminated according to Coombs' procedure in the first round and thereafter *c* (the abstainers' top preference!) is elected thereby demonstrating the vulnerability of Coombs' procedure to the No–Show Paradox.

This example can also be used to demonstrate the vulnerability of Coombs' procedure to the Truncation Paradox: if the two voters with preference ordering $c \succ b \succ a$ decide to list only their top preference then, *ceteris paribus*, *b* would be eliminated according to Coombs' procedure and thereafter *c* would be elected!

If, *ceteris paribus*, all voters invert their preference orderings, then we obtain the following distribution of votes:

No. of voters	Preference orderings
4	$c \succ b \succ a$
4	$a \succ c \succ b$
5	$b \succ a \succ c$
2	$a \succ b \succ c$

As no candidate obtains an absolute majority of the votes in the first counting round, *c* is eliminated and thereafter *b* is elected in the second counting round—thus demonstrating the vulnerability of Coombs' procedure to the Preference Inversion Paradox.

5.3.7 *Reinforcement Paradox*

Example 5.3.7.1 demonstrates the vulnerability of Coombs' procedure to the Reinforcement Paradox.

5.3.7.1 Example

Suppose there are two districts, I and II. In district I there are 34 voters whose preference orderings among three candidates, a, b, and c, are as follows:

No. of voters	Preference orderings
9	$a \succ b \succ c$
9	$b \succ c \succ a$
11	$c \succ a \succ b$
5	$c \succ b \succ a$

and in district II there are 7 voters whose preference orderings among the three candidates are as follows:

No. of voters	Preference orderings
1	$a \succ b \succ c$
6	$b \succ a \succ c$

Since no candidate is ranked first by an absolute majority of the voters in district I, candidate a is eliminated under Coombs' procedure in the first round, and thereafter candidate b is elected. In district II candidate b is ranked first by an absolute majority of the voters and is elected right away.

However, if, *ceteris paribus*, the two districts are amalgamated into a single district of 41 voters then one obtains the following distribution of preferences:

No. of voters	Preference orderings
10	$a \succ b \succ c$
6	$b \succ a \succ c$
9	$b \succ c \succ a$
11	$c \succ a \succ b$
5	$c \succ b \succ a$

Since none of the three candidates is ranked first by an absolute majority of the voters in the amalgamated district, candidate c is eliminated according to Coombs' procedure in the first round, and candidate a (rather than b) is elected thereafter—thus demonstrating the vulnerability of Coombs' procedure to the Reinforcement Paradox.

5.3.8 Twin Paradox

Example 5.3.8.1 demonstrates the vulnerability of Coombs' procedure to the Twin Paradox.

5.3.8.1 Example

Suppose there are 20 voters who have to choose one out of four candidates, *a*, *b*, *c*, or *d*, under Coombs' procedure and whose preference orderings among these candidates are as follows:

No. of voters	Preference orderings
5	$a \succ b \succ d \succ c$
5	$b \succ c \succ d \succ a$
1	$b \succ a \succ d \succ c$
6	$c \succ a \succ d \succ b$
1	$c \succ b \succ a \succ d$
2	$c \succ b \succ d \succ a$

Since no voter is ranked first by an absolute majority of the voters, candidate *a* is eliminated according to Coombs' procedure in the first round and thereafter *b* is elected.

Now suppose that, *ceteris paribus*, two more voters with preference ordering $b \succ a \succ d \succ c$ join the electorate thereby apparently increasing the chances of candidate *b* to be elected. However, as result of this increase of the electorate candidate *c* (rather than *a*) will be eliminated in the first round under Coombs' procedure, and thereafter a tie will be created between candidates *a* and *b*—thereby *decreasing* the chances of candidate *b* to be elected if the tie is to be broken randomly.

5.3.9 *SCC Paradox*

Example 5.3.9.1 demonstrates the vulnerability of Coombs' procedure to SCC.

5.3.9.1 Example

Suppose that there are 29 voters having to elect under Coombs' procedure one out of four candidates, *a*, *b*, *c*, or *d*, and whose preference orderings among the four candidates are as follows:

No. of voters	Preference orderings
11	$a \succ b \succ c \succ d$
12	$b \succ c \succ d \succ a$
2	$b \succ a \succ d \succ c$
4	$c \succ a \succ d \succ b$

Since none of the candidates is ranked first by an absolute majority of the voters, one deletes according to Coombs' procedure the candidate who is ranked last by the largest number of voters. In the above example this candidate is *a*. After deleting *a* candidate *b* is ranked first by an absolute majority of the voters and is elected.

Now suppose that, *ceteris paribus*, candidate *c* drops out of the race. As a result candidate *a* is ranked first by an absolute majority of the voters and is elected—contrary to SCC.

5.4 The (In)Vulnerability of Bucklin's Procedure to Various Paradoxes

5.4.1 *Condorcet Winner Paradox*

Example 5.3.1.1 above can be used to demonstrate the susceptibility of Bucklin's procedure to the Condorcet Winner Paradox. In this example *b* is the Condorcet Winner but under Bucklin's procedure *c* is elected because the number of voters (33) who rank *c* first or second exceeds the number of voters (32) who rank *a* first or second, as well as the number of voters (25) who rank *b* first or second.

5.4.2 *Absolute Majority Winner Paradox*

Bucklin's procedure always elects a candidate who is listed first in the preference orderings of an absolute majority of the voters. Therefore, Bucklin's procedure is invulnerable to this paradox.

5.4.3 *Condorcet Loser Paradox*

Example 5.4.3.1 demonstrates that a Condorcet Loser may be elected under Bucklin's procedure.

5.4.3.1 Example

This example is due to Tideman (2006, p. 197, Example 13.13). Suppose there are 29 voters whose preference orderings among four candidates, *w*, *x*, *y*, *z*, are as follows:

No. of voters	Preference orderings
5	$w \succ x \succ y \succ z$
3	$w \succ z \succ x \succ y$

(continued)

(continued)

No. of voters	Preference orderings
5	$x \succ y \succ w \succ z$
2	$x \succ z \succ y \succ w$
3	$y \succ w \succ x \succ z$
2	$y \succ z \succ w \succ x$
4	$z \succ w \succ x \succ y$
2	$z \succ x \succ y \succ w$
3	$z \succ y \succ w \succ x$

The social preference ordering here contains a top cycle $(w \succ x \succ y \succ w) \succ z$, but since each of the three candidates w, x, y beats candidate z in pairwise contests, candidate z is a Condorcet Loser. However, under Bucklin's procedure candidate z will be elected because the number of voters (16) who rank z first or second in their preference ordering exceeds the number of voters who rank any of the other three candidates in first or second place in their preference ordering.

5.4.4 *Absolute Majority Loser Paradox*

Although Bucklin's procedure can elect a Condorcet Loser, it cannot elect an Absolute Majority Loser. This is so because an Absolute Majority Loser is, by definition, an alternative that is ranked last by at least an absolute majority of the voters. This implies, in turn, that such an alternative cannot be elected according to Bucklin's procedure because the sum of its top + second + third + ··· + penultimate ranks, must be smaller than the absolute majority of the voters.

5.4.5 *Pareto-Dominated Candidate Paradox*

An alternative, x, is Pareto-dominated by another alternative, y, if *all* voters rank y higher than x. So if x is Pareto-dominated by y then x cannot be elected under Bucklin's procedure because y's sum of top + second + third + ··· + penultimate ranks will reach an amount which is at least equal to an absolute majority of the voters before this sum will be reached by x, hence it cannot happen under Bucklin's procedure that x is elected but y is not elected.

5.4.6 *Lack of Monotonicity Paradox*

Bucklin's procedure is not vulnerable to lack of monotonicity in *fixed electorates*. This is so because if alternative x has been originally elected then, *ceteris paribus*,

x will be elected *a fortiori* if some voters will change their minds and rank x higher in their preference ordering. However, Bucklin's procedure may exhibit monotonicity failure if, *ceteris paribus*, additional voters join the electorate who rank x at the top of their preference ordering. For examples of such monotonicity failure see Felsenthal and Nurmi (2016, 2017).

5.4.7 Reinforcement Paradox

Example 5.4.7.1 demonstrates the vulnerability of Bucklin's procedure to the Reinforcement Paradox.

5.4.7.1 Example

This example is due to Tideman (2006, p. 205, Example 13.19). Suppose there are two districts, I and II. In District I there are 15 voters whose preference ordering among three candidates, a, b, c, are as follows:

No. of voters	Preference orderings
6	$a \succ c \succ b$
5	$b \succ a \succ c$
4	$c \succ b \succ a$

and in district II there are 9 voters whose preference orderings among the same three candidates are as follows:

No. of voters	Preference ordering
5	$a \succ b \succ c$
4	$c \succ b \succ a$

Given these data a will be elected under Bucklin's procedure in district I (in the second counting round with 11 votes), as well as in district II (in the first counting round with 5 votes).

However if, *ceteris paribus*, the two districts are amalgamated into a single district, we obtain a district of 24 voters with the following preference orderings among the three candidates:

No. of voters	Preference ordering
5	$a \succ b \succ c$
6	$a \succ c \succ b$
5	$b \succ a \succ c$
8	$c \succ b \succ a$

In this amalgamated district candidate b will be elected under Bucklin's procedure (in the second counting round with 18 votes)—in violation of the Reinforcement axiom.

5.4.8 No–Show, Twin, Truncation, and SCC Paradoxes

Example 5.4.8.1 demonstrates the susceptibility of Bucklin's procedure to the No–Show, Twin, and Truncation paradoxes.

5.4.8.1 Example

Suppose there are 101 voters whose preference orderings among four candidates, a, b, c, and d, are as follows:

No. of voters	Preference orderings
43	$a \succ b \succ c \succ d$
26	$b \succ c \succ d \succ a$
15	$c \succ d \succ b \succ a$
17	$d \succ a \succ b \succ c$

If one of the four candidates must be elected under Bucklin's procedure then candidate b would be elected because the number of voters (69) who rank b first or second in their preference ordering exceeds the number of voters who rank any of the other candidates in first or second place in their preference ordering.

Now suppose that *ceteris paribus*, 16 of the 17 voters whose top preference is d decide not to participate in the election. As a result candidate a would be elected because an absolute majority of the voters (43) rank a as their top preference. This result is preferable for all the voters whose top preference is d who thus obtain their second preference (instead of their third preference)—thereby demonstrating simultaneously both the No–Show and Twin Paradoxes.

To demonstrate the vulnerability of Bucklin's procedure to the Truncation Paradox suppose that the 43 voters whose top preference is a decide to list only their top preference. In this case a would be listed first or second by 60 voters—which is more than any other voter is listed first or second—thereby a is elected under Bucklin's procedure, an outcome which these 43 voters prefer to the election of b.

This example can also be used to demonstrate the vulnerability of Bucklin's procedure to the SCC Paradox. We just saw that in this example candidate b is elected (with 69 votes in the second counting round) under Bucklin's procedure when all four candidates and 101 voters participate in the election. However, *ceteris paribus*, a is elected under Bucklin's procedure (in the first counting round with 60 votes) if candidate d drops out of the race—thereby demonstrating the violation of the SCC postulate.

5.4.9 *Preference Inversion Paradox*

Example 5.4.9.1 demonstrates the vulnerability of Bucklin's procedure to the Preference Inversion Paradox.

5.4.9.1 Example

Suppose that there are four voters whose preference orderings among five candidates, a, b, c, d, and e, are as follows:

No. of voters	Preference orderings
2	$a \succ d \succ b \succ e \succ c$
2	$e \succ c \succ b \succ a \succ d$

If one of the five candidates must be elected under Bucklin's procedure then candidate b would be elected because the number of voters (4) who rank b first, second, or third in their preference ordering exceeds the number of voters who rank any of the other candidates in first, second or third place in their preference ordering.

Now suppose that, *ceteris paribus*, all voters invert their preference orderings among the five candidates. In this case b, who is placed in the middle of all candidates' preference orderings, would still be elected—thus demonstrating the vulnerability of Bucklin's procedure to the Preference Inversion Paradox.

5.5 The (In)Vulnerability of the Range Voting (RV) Procedure to Various Paradoxes

In contrast to all other voting procedures except Majority Judgment (MJ) where a necessary condition to demonstrate the paradoxes afflicting them is that there exist at least three candidates, it is possible to demonstrate most of the paradoxes afflicting the RV (and MJ) procedure when there are just two candidates.

5.5.1 *Condorcet Winner, Absolute Majority Winner, Condorcet Loser, and Absolute Majority Loser Paradoxes*

Example 5.5.1.1 demonstrates the vulnerability of the RV procedure to all these four paradoxes.

5.5.1.1 Example

Suppose there are five voters, V_1, V_2, V_3, V_4, and V_5, who award the following (cardinal) grades on a scale from 1 (lowest) to 10 (highest) to two candidates, *x* and *y*:

Candidates/voters	V_1	V_2	V_3	V_4	V_5	Mean grade
x	2	2	2	3	10	3.8
y	1	1	1	10	7	4.0

As the mean grade of candidate *y* is higher than that of candidate *x*, candidate *y* is elected by the RV procedure. However, note that an absolute majority of the voters (V_1, V_2, V_3, V_5) awarded candidate *x* a higher grade than they awarded to candidate *y*, and an absolute majority of the voters (V_1, V_2, and V_3) awarded *y* the lowest grade. Hence candidate *x* is not only a Condorcet Winner but also an Absolute Majority Winner, whereas candidate *y* is not only a Condorcet Loser but also an Absolute Majority Loser.

5.5.2 *Pareto-Dominated Candidate Paradox*

If candidate *x* is Pareto-dominated by candidate *y*, its mean score is strictly smaller than that of the latter because each voter assigns to *y* a larger cardinal value than to *x*. Hence a Pareto-dominated candidate cannot be elected by the Range Voting procedure.

5.5.3 *Lack of Monotonicity Paradox*

If candidate *x* is the Range Voting winner in a given profile then its score will be strictly larger in the profile obtained from the original one by improving *x*'s position, *ceteris paribus*, since at least one voter gives *x* a larger value than previously, while no other candidate gets a larger value than previously. Thus, *x* remains the Range Voting winner in the new profile. The same holds for all profiles where the original profile is augmented by voters ranking *x* first. Thus, the range voting procedure is monotonic both in fixed and variable electorates.

5.5.4 *Reinforcement Paradox*

Suppose that the electorate is divided into two or more subsets with empty intersection and suppose, moreover, that *x* is the Range Voting winner in each subset. This means that the scores of *x* are the largest in every subset of voters. Thus, the

Range Voting score of x must also be the largest when the scores are determined on the basis of the sum of scores that each candidate receives in each subset.

5.5.5 *No–Show Paradox*

If x is the Range Voting winner in a profile, no voter ranking x first can improve the outcome by abstaining since by so doing he/she decreases the score of x thereby possibly making it a non–winner. Furthermore, if x is the Range Voting winner, no candidate y can become the winner in circumstances where a group of voters ranking y last joins the electorate. This is because y receives less value from the new entrants than any other alternative including x. Hence the sum of values for x must remain higher than those received by y. Therefore, y cannot become the winner in the new profile. (This does not say that x remains the winner in the new profile, only that y isn't.)

5.5.6 *Twin Paradox*

According to the Twin Paradox two voters having the same preference ordering may obtain a preferable outcome if, *ceteris paribus*, one of them decides not to participate in the election while the other votes sincerely for his/her top preference. This paradox cannot occur under the Range Voting procedure because if alternative x constitutes the top preference of the first twin and is the winner under this procedure (because it gained the largest mean score), then, *ceteris paribus*, x would remain the winner with an even larger mean score if an additional twin joins the electorate who votes for x.

5.5.7 *Truncation Paradox*

Example 5.5.7.1 demonstrates the vulnerability of the RV procedure to the Truncation Paradox.

5.5.7.1 Example

Suppose there are seven voters, V_1–V_7, who award the following (cardinal) grades on a scale of 1 (lowest) to 10 (highest) to two candidates, x and y:

Candidates/voters	V_1	V_2	V_3	V_4	V_5	V_6	V_7	Mean grade
x	1	1	1	10	5	4	7	4.143
y	2	2	2	3	8	5	8	4.286

As the mean grade of candidate y is higher than that of candidate x, candidate y is elected by the RV procedure. However, as voter V_4 grades candidate x higher than y s/he is not satisfied with this result and will be better off if s/he does not grade candidate y at all, thereby demonstrating the vulnerability of the RV procedure to the Truncation Paradox. (*Ceteris paribus*, if voter V_4 does not grade candidate y then this candidate will be deemed to have been awarded the lowest grade (1) by voter V_4 and, as a result, the average grade of candidate y will drop to 4.0 thus electing candidate x.)

5.5.8 *The SCC Paradox*

The Subset Choice Condition requires that the winner in a profile should remain the winner when some other candidate(s) is (are) removed from the candidate set, *ceteris paribus*. Failing this means that the procedure under investigation does not satisfy the Subset Choice Condition. Since the Range Voting system operates on cardinal grade values given by voters to candidates, removing a set of candidates does not change the distribution of grade sums among the remaining ones. Hence, the winners remain winners after any removals of non–winners. Thus, the Subset Choice Condition is satisfied by Range Voting.

5.5.9 *Preference Inversion Paradox*

Example 5.5.9.1 demonstrates the vulnerability of the RV procedure to the Preference Inversion Paradox.

5.5.9.1 Example

Suppose there are seven voters V_1–V_7, who award the following (cardinal) grades on a scale of 0 (lowest) to 7 (highest) to three candidates, x, y and z:

Candidates/voters	V_1	V_2	V_3	V_4	V_5	V_6	V_7	Mean grade
x	7	7	7	0	0	0	0	3
y	1	1	1	7	7	1	1	2.714
z	0	0	0	1	1	7	7	2.286

Since candidate x has the highest mean grade, this candidate is the RV winner.

Now suppose that all the seven voters invert the grades they awarded to the three candidates. As a result we obtain the following distribution of grades:

Candidates/voters	V_1	V_2	V_3	V_4	V_5	V_6	V_7	Mean grade
x	0	0	0	7	7	7	7	4
y	1	1	1	0	0	1	1	0.714
z	7	7	7	1	1	0	0	3.286

In this table we see that despite the inversion of grades, candidate x has still the highest mean grade—thereby demonstrating the vulnerability of the RV procedure to the Preference Inversion Paradox.

5.6 The (In)Vulnerability of the Majority Judgment (MJ) Procedure to Various Paradoxes

The paradoxes afflicting the Majority Judgment (MJ) procedure are discussed at length in Felsenthal and Machover (2008).

5.6.1 Condorcet Winner, Absolute Majority Winner, Condorcet Loser, and Absolute Majority Loser Paradoxes

Example 5.6.1.1 demonstrates the vulnerability of the MJ procedure to all these four paradoxes.

5.6.1.1 Example

This example is due to Felsenthal and Machover (2008, p. 330). Suppose there are three voters, V_1, V_2, and V_3, who award the following (ordinal) grades (on a scale of A–H with A the lowest and H the highest grade) to two candidates, x and y:

Candidate/voter	V_1	V_2	V_3	Median grade
x	B	C	H	C
y	A	F	G	F

As the median grade of candidate y is higher than that of candidate x, candidate y is elected by the MJ procedure. However, note that an absolute majority of the voters (V_1 and V_3) awarded candidate y a lower grade than they awarded candidate *x*—hence candidate *x* is not only a Condorcet Winner but also an Absolute Majority Winner, whereas candidate *y* is not only a Condorcet Loser but also an Absolute Majority Loser.

5.6.2 *Pareto-Dominated Candidate Paradox*

If *x* Pareto-dominates *y* in terms of ordinal grades, i.e., if all voters assign to *x* a higher ordinal grade than to *y*, then the median grade of *y* cannot be higher than that of *x*. Thus, it cannot be the case that *y* is elected by the MJ procedure while *x* isn't.

5.6.3 *Lack of Monotonicity Paradox*

Suppose that *x* is the MJ winner and that its grades are increased by some voters, *ceteris paribus*. Then it must remain the winner in the new profile since *x*'s median grade is at least as high as it was at the outset, while the grades of all other voters are unchanged. So, *x* is the MJ winner also in the new profile. This applies only to fixed electorates. Under variable electorates MJ is vulnerable to monotonicity paradoxes (see Felsenthal and Nurmi 2016, 2017).

5.6.4 *The Reinforcement Paradox*

Example 5.6.4.1 demonstrates the vulnerability of the MJ procedure to the Reinforcement Paradox.

5.6.4.1 Example

This example is due to Felsenthal and Machover (2008, p. 327).

Suppose there are three regions, I, II, and III, in each of which 101 voters grade each of two candidates, *x* and *y*, on an ordinal scale A–D. The following lists show the distributions of grades. The figure next to a grade is the number of voters awarding that grade.

Region I:				
x:	21A	31B	48C	1D
y:	40A	11B	48C	2D

Region II:

x:	1A	46B	14C	40D
y:	1A	45B	33C	22D

Region III:

x:	40B	20C	41D
y:	48B	3C	50D

In all three elections the two candidates have equal median grades (median grade B in region I and median grade C in regions II, III), so the tie–breaking algorithm proposed by Balinski and Laraki (2007, 2011) must be used. The number of iterations required for breaking the tie in each of the three regions are 2, 7, and 2, respectively, whereupon *y* wins in each of the three regions.[3]

However, if the three regions are amalgamated into a single region we obtain the following distribution of grades awarded to candidates *x* and *y* by the 303 voters:

Amalgamated region:

x:	22A	117B	82C	82D
y:	41A	104B	84C	74D

Here again candidates *x* and *y* obtain the same median grade (C), but when one breaks this tie (after 13 iterations) *x* wins—in violation of the Reinforcement postulate.

5.6.5 *The No–Show and Twin Paradoxes*

Example 5.6.5.1 demonstrates the vulnerability of the MJ procedure to the No–Show and Twin Paradoxes.

5.6.5.1 Example

This example is due to Felsenthal and Machover (2008, p. 329).

[3]To break a tie between two leading candidates who have the same median grade, one performs one or more iterations in each of which the equal median grade of the two candidates is dropped. This process continues until one reaches a situation where the candidates' median grades are no longer the same. If no such situation is reached then the tie is broken randomly. With an even number of grades Balinski and Laraki take the median to be the lower of the two middle grades.

Suppose that seven voters, V_1–V_7, grade two candidates, *x* and *y*, on an ordinal scale ranging between A and F, as follows:

Candidate/voter	V_1	V_2	V_3	V_4	V_5	V_6	V_7	Median grade
x	A	A	A	D	E	E	F	D
y	B	B	B	C	F	F	F	C

Here *x* wins. But now suppose that voters V_1 and V_2, both of whom awarded the same grades as voter V_3, and who prefer candidate *y*, abstain from voting. Then we get:

Candidate/voter	V_3	V_4	V_5	V_6	V_7	Median grade
x	A	D	E	E	F	E
y	B	C	F	F	F	F

Here *y* wins. Thus by abstaining voters V_1 and V_2 cause their favorite candidate to win—thereby demonstrating the vulnerability of the MJ procedure to the No-Show Paradox. Similarly, since V_3 prefers candidate *y* to *x*, one could expect that if, *ceteris paribus*, the two "twins" (V_1 and V_2)—who grade the two candidates in the same way as V_3—would join the electorate, then *y* would certainly be elected. However, as can be seen from the first table, in this case *x* would be elected, thereby demonstrating the vulnerability of the MJ procedure to the Twin Paradox.

5.6.6 *Truncation Paradox*

Example 5.6.6.1 demonstrates the vulnerability of the MJ procedure to the Truncation Paradox.

5.6.6.1 Example

Suppose there are seven voters, V_1–V_7, who award the following (ordinal) grades (on a scale of A–J) to two candidates, *x* and *y*:

Candidate/voter	V_1	V_2	V_3	V_4	V_5	V_6	V_7	Median grade
x	A	A	A	J	E	D	G	D
y	B	B	B	C	H	E	H	C

Here *x* is elected because his/her median grade is higher than that of *y*. Voter V_6 does not like this result so if, *ceteris paribus*, s/he decides to grade only candidate *y*, then candidate *x* would be deemed to have been awarded the lowest grade (A) by V_6 and, consequently, candidate *x*'s median grade would drop from D to A—causing candidate y to be elected. Voter V_6 of course prefers this result—thereby demonstrating the vulnerability of the MJ procedure to the Truncation Paradox.

5.6.7 *The SCC Paradox*

The grades assigned to candidates by voters remain the same in the original alternative set and its subsets. So, if x's median grade is the highest in the whole set of candidates, it is also the highest in each subset of candidates that includes x.

5.6.8 *The Preference Inversion Paradox*

Example 5.6.8.1 demonstrates the vulnerability of the MJ procedure to the Preference Inversion Paradox.

5.6.8.1 Example

Suppose there are three voters, V_1–V_3, who award the following (ordinal) grades on a scale of A (lowest) to G (highest) to three candidates, x, y and z:

Candidate/voter	V_1	V_2	V_3	median grade
x	A	G	D	D
y	E	E	C	E
z	F	C	A	C

Since candidate y has the highest median grade, this candidate is the MJ winner.

Now suppose that all the three voters invert the grades they awarded to the three candidates. As a result we obtain the following distribution of grades:

Candidate/voter	V_1	V_2	V_3	Median grade
x	F	C	A	C
y	E	E	C	E
z	A	G	D	D

Thus we see that despite the inversion of grades, candidate y has still the highest median grade and hence remains the MJ winner—thereby demonstrating the vulnerability of the MJ procedure to the Preference Inversion Paradox.

The summary of the preceding discussion is presented in Table 5.1.

Table 5.1 (In)Vulnerability of ranked non condorcet–consistent voting procedures to 13 voting paradoxes

Paradox	Procedure					
	Borda	Alternative Vote (AV) STV	Coombs	Bucklin	Range Voting	Majority Judgment
Condorcet Winner Paradox	+	+	+	+	+	+
Absolute Majority Winner Paradox	⊕	–	–	–	⊕	⊕
Condorcet Loser Paradox	–	–	–	⊕	⊕	⊕
Absolute Majority Loser Paradox	–	–	–	–	⊕	⊕
Pareto Dominated Candidate	–	–	–	–	–	–
Lack of Monotonicity	–	⊕	⊕	–	–	–
Reinforcement	–	+	+	+	–	+
No–show	–	+	+	+	–	+
Twin	–	+	+	+	–	+
Truncation	+	+	+	+	+	+
Subset Choice Condition (SCC)	+	+	+	+	–	–
Preference Inversion	–	+	+	+	+	+
Dependence on Order of Voting (DOV)	–	–	–	–	–	–
Total ⊕ signs	1	1	1	1	3	3
Total + and ⊕ signs	4	8	8	8	6	9

Notes
A + sign indicates that a procedure is vulnerable to the specified paradox;
A ⊕ sign indicates that a procedure is vulnerable to the specified paradox which seems to us an especially intolerable paradox;
A – sign indicates that a procedure is not vulnerable to the specified paradox;
It is assumed that all voters have linear preference ordering among all competing candidates.

Exercises

Problem 5.1 A ranking R of ν voters together with its reversal R′ of ν voters is called a *reversal component* by Saari. Show that adding such a component to any 3–alternative profile leaves the Borda ranking of the alternatives unchanged. Show that adding such a component to a 3–alternative profile, may change the Plurality Voting winner. Illustrate using the following profile.

No. of voters	Preference ordering
4	$a \succ b \succ c$
3	$b \succ c \succ a$
2	$c \succ b \succ a$

Problem 5.2 Consider the following procedure: given the profile of voter preference rankings, give each alternative ranked first by a voter 1 point, each alternative ranked second 2 points etc. Now, sum up the points given to each alternative and form the collective ranking on the basis of the sum of scores of the alternatives so that those with larger scores are ranked higher than those with lower scores. How does this method relate to the Borda count? How could this method be modified to end up with a system that always ends up with the same results as the Borda count?

Problem 5.3 Determine the winner according to the Majority Judgment (MJ) procedure given that the following five voters, 1–5, assign ordinal grades on a scale from A (lowest) to F (highest) to three alternatives, x, y, z.

Alternative\voter	1	2	3	4	5
X	C	C	C	F	F
Y	D	A	A	D	D
Z	B	F	B	B	E

Problem 5.4 Assign to grades A–F in Problem 5.3 numerical values (or scores) from 1 to 6, respectively. Then compute the sum of scores for each alternative and determine which alternative is the winner if the winner is the alternative which has the highest sum. How does the result differ from the MJ outcome?

Answers to Exercises

Problem 5.1 Let the ranking R be $a \succ b \succ c$ and let the R′ ranking be $c \succ b \succ a$. Then a's total Borda score is added by $2v$ points, b's by $v + v = 2v$ points, and c's by $2v$ points. Hence the differences between the Borda scores remain the same as before adding the reversal component.

Adding such a component to a 3–alternative profile may change the Plurality Voting winner if before the addition of the reversal component there was a tie between a and b, it is broken in a's favor when the reversal component is added. Thus, if we add to the (original) profile 4 voters with $c \succ a \succ b$ ranking and 4 voters with its reversal, then the resulting profile gets the following form:

No. of voters	Preference orderings
4	$a \succ b \succ c$
3	$b \succ c \succ a$
2	$c \succ b \succ a$
4	$c \succ a \succ b$
4	$b \succ a \succ c$

Thus b is the Plurality Voting winner.

Problem 5.2 This system of assigning points to alternatives results in a social preference ordering which is the reverse of that obtained under Borda's procedure. To obtain the same social preference ordering as that obtained under Borda's procedure one must reverse the order of preference in the social preference ordering, i.e., the alternative with the smallest score should be ranked first and that with the largest score should be ranked last.

Problem 5.3 The median grades of alternatives x, y, z are C, D, and B, respectively, so alternative y wins.

Problem 5.4 If one replaces the grades A–F by the numbers 1–6, respectively, then the sum of x's grades is 21, that of y is 14, and that of z is 17, so x wins.

References

Balinski, M., & Laraki, R. (2007). A theory of measuring, electing and ranking. *Proceedings of the National Academy of Sciences of the United States of America (PNAS), 104*, 8720–8725.

Balinski, M., & Laraki, R. (2011). *Majority judgment: Measuring, ranking, and electing*. Cambridge, MA: MIT Press.

Coombs, C. H. (1964). *A theory of data*. New York: Wiley.

Felsenthal, D. S. (2012). Review of paradoxes afflicting procedures for electing a single candidate. In D. S. Felsenthal & M. Machover (Eds.), *Electoral systems: Paradoxes, assumptions, and procedures* (pp. 19–92). Berlin Heidelberg: Springer, Chapter 3.

Felsenthal, D. S., & Machover, M. (2008). The majority judgement voting procedure: A critical evaluation. *Homo Oeconomicus, 25,* 319–333.

Felsenthal, D. S., & Nurmi, H. (2016). Two types of participation failure under nine voting methods in variable electorates. *Public Choice, 168,* 115–135.

Felsenthal, D. S., & Nurmi, H. (2017). *Monotonicity failures afflicting procedures for electing a single candidate*. Cham, Switzerland: Springer.

Fishburn, P. C. (1974). Paradoxes of voting. *American Political Science Review, 68,* 537–546.

Saari, D. G., & Barney, S. (2003). Consequences of reversing the preferences. *Mathematical Intelligencer, 25,* 17–31.

Smith, J. H. (1973). Aggregation of preferences with variable electorate. *Econometrica, 41,* 1027–1041.

Tideman, N. (2006). *Collective decisions and voting: The potential for public choice*. Aldershot, Hampshire, England: Ashgate Publishing Ltd.

Chapter 6
The (In)Vulnerability of the Ranked Condorcet–Consistent Procedures to Various Paradoxes

Abstract We study the vulnerability or invulnerability of eight voting procedures (Minimax, Dodgson's, Nanson's, Copeland's, Black's, Kemeny's, Schwartz's and Young's procedures) to 13 voting paradoxes. The invulnerabilities are explained and the vulnerabilities demonstrated through illustrative profiles where the paradoxes occur under the procedures examined.

Keywords Ranked voting procedures · Condorcet consistent procedures · Voting paradoxes · Vulnerability to paradoxes

6.1 The (In)Vulnerability of the Minimax Procedure (aka Simpson–Kramer or Condorcet's Procedure) to Various Paradoxes

6.1.1 Condorcet Winner Paradox

The Minimax procedure is invulnerable to the Condorcet Winner Paradox. Suppose that there is a Condorcet Winner, say x, in the profile. This means that in the pairwise comparison matrix[1] the row representing x has all non-diagonal entries

---

This chapter is partly based on Felsenthal (2012) and partly on Nurmi (2012).

All the procedures surveyed in this chapter are invulnerable to the Dependence on Order of Voting (DOV) Paradox (cf. Chap. 2) because under these procedures all candidates are voted upon simultaneously rather than sequentially.

---

[1]A pairwise comparison matrix is a matrix with n rows and n columns (where n is the number of candidates). In such a matrix the entry in row x and column y denotes the number of voters who rank candidate x ahead of candidate y in their preference ordering and the entry in row y and column x is the complementary number denoting the number of voters who rank candidate y ahead of candidate x. The cells along the main diagonal of this matrix are left empty.

D. S. Felsenthal and H. Nurmi, *Voting Procedures for Electing a Single Candidate*, SpringerBriefs in Economics, https://doi.org/10.1007/978-3-319-74033-1_6

strictly larger than $v/2$ (with v denoting the number of voters). By symmetry in the column representing x all non-diagonal entries must be strictly less than $v/2$. This means that the minimum entry in the row representing x is strictly larger than $v/2$, while the minimum entry in every other row is strictly smaller than $v/2$. Hence the Minimax procedure selects the Condorcet Winner, and it only, in every profile in which it exists.

6.1.2 *Condorcet Loser, Absolute Majority Loser and Preference Inversion Paradoxes*

The Minimax procedure is vulnerable to the Condorcet Loser, Absolute Majority Loser, and Preference Inversion Paradoxes. Example 6.1.2.1 demonstrates this.

6.1.2.1 Example

Suppose there are 11 voters whose preference orderings among four candidates, *a, b, c, d*, are as follows:

No. of voters	Preference orderings
2	$d \succ a \succ c \succ b$
3	$d \succ b \succ a \succ c$
3	$c \succ b \succ a \succ d$
1	$b \succ a \succ c \succ d$
2	$a \succ c \succ b \succ d$

This preference profile can be depicted as the following paired comparison matrix.

	a	*b*	*c*	*d*
a	–	4	8	6
b	7	–	4	6
c	3	7	–	6
d	5	5	5	–

As can be seen from the paired comparisons matrix, the social preference ordering in Example 6.1.2.1 contains a top cycle $[b \succ a \succ c \succ b] \succ d$, i.e., *d* is the Condorcet Loser which happens to be also an Absolute Majority Loser. However, the Minimax procedure will elect *d* because *d*'s worst loss margin (6) is smaller than the worst loss margin of each of the other three candidates (7, 7, 8 for *a, b, c*, respectively). Hence the Minimax procedure is vulnerable to the Absolute Majority Loser Paradox.

This example can also be used to demonstrate the vulnerability of the Minimax procedure to the Preference Inversion Paradox. If all voters invert their preference orderings then *d* becomes an Absolute Majority Winner and hence is elected under the Minimax procedure.

6.1.3 The SCC Paradox

Example 6.1.3.1 demonstrates the vulnerability of the Minimax procedure to SCC.

6.1.3.1 Example

This example is due to Fishburn (1974, p. 540). Suppose there are seven voters who are divided into three groups who have to select under the Minimax procedure one out of four candidates, *a, b, c,* or *d*, and whose preference orderings among these candidates are as follows:

Group	No. of voters	Preference orderings
G1	3	$d \succ c \succ b \succ a$
G2	2	$a \succ d \succ c \succ b$
G3	2	$b \succ a \succ d \succ c$

From this preference list we see that the social preference ordering is cyclical ($a \succ d \succ c \succ b \succ a$). It can be depicted as a (cyclical) paired comparisons matrix as follows:

	a	b	c	d
a	–	2	4	4
b	5	–	2	2
c	3	5	–	0
d	3	5	7	–

From this matrix we can see that the worst loss of candidate *a* is 5 (against candidate *b*), the worst loss of candidate *b* is also 5 (against candidates *c, d*), the worst loss of candidate *c* is 7 (against candidate *d*) and the worst loss of candidate *d* is 4 (against candidate *a*). As candidate *d*'s loss is the smallest, this candidate would be elected under the Minimax procedure.

Now suppose that, *ceteris paribus*, candidate *b* drops out of the race. In this case candidate *a* becomes the Absolute Majority Winner and will be elected under the Minimax procedure—in violation of SCC.

6.1.4 Absolute Majority Winner Paradox

The Minimax procedure avoids the Absolute Majority Winner Paradox since the candidate ranked first by an absolute majority of voters is a special case of a Condorcet Winner. Hence, the argument just presented shows that no other alternative than the Absolute Majority Winner can be elected.

6.1.5 Pareto-Dominated Candidate Paradox

Suppose that *x* is Pareto-dominated by *y*. Then all entries on the row representing *x* in the pairwise comparison matrix are smaller than or equal to the corresponding entries on *y*'s row. (N.B. the minimum entry on *x*'s row is 0, since by assumption no voter prefers *x* to *y*.) In particular, the minimum entry on *x*'s row cannot be larger than the minimal entry on *y*'s row. Hence, it cannot be the case that *x* is elected and *y* is not under the Minimax procedure. Thus, the Minimax procedure avoids this paradox.

6.1.6 Lack of Monotonicity Paradox

The Minimax procedure is invulnerable to any form of monotonicity failure. This is so because if *x*, the candidate elected originally, is a Condorcet Winner, then *x* remains a Condorcet Winner and consequently the Minimax Winner if, *ceteris paribus*, some of the voters who originally ranked *x* lower in their preference ordering will now change their minds and rank *x* higher in their preference ordering, or if, *ceteris paribus*, additional voters join the electorate who rank *x* at the top of their preference ordering. And if *x* was not originally the Condorcet Winner then the fact that, *ceteris paribus*, some voters raised *x* in their preference orderings or that additional voters joined the electorate whose top preference is *x* must either cause *x* to become a Condorcet Winner or further reduce *x*'s worst loss—thereby *x* must remain the Minimax winner. Similarly, if *x* was not originally a winner then the fact that, *ceteris paribus*, some voters lowered *x* in their preference orderings or that additional voters joined the electorate whose bottom preference is *x* must further increase *x*'s worst loss—thereby *x* must remain the Minimax non–winner.

6.1.7 Reinforcement Paradox

Example 6.1.7.1 demonstrates the vulnerability of the Minimax procedure to the Reinforcement Paradox.

6.1.7.1 Example

Suppose there are two districts, one with 11 voters whose preference orderings among four candidates are as in Example 6.1.2.1 and a second district with three voters two of whom have preference ordering $d \succ a \succ b \succ c$ and the third voter has preference ordering $b \succ a \succ c \succ d$.

As we have seen in Example 6.1.2.1, candidate *d* will be elected in the first district, and as candidate *d* is the Absolute Majority Winner in the second district s/he will also be elected in the second district under the Minimax procedure.

Now suppose that, *ceteris paribus*, these two districts are amalgamated into one district of 14 voters having the following paired comparisons matrix:

	a	*b*	*c*	*d*
a	–	6	11	7
b	8	–	7	7
c	3	7	–	7
d	7	7	7	–

From this paired comparisons matrix it is easy to see that there is a tie between candidates *b* and *d* because the largest loss of both of them is smallest (7), thus according to the Minimax procedure a lottery should be conducted between them—thereby demonstrating the vulnerability of the Minimax procedure to the Reinforcement Paradox.

6.1.8 No-Show and Twin Paradoxes

Example 6.1.8.1 demonstrates the vulnerability of the Minimax procedure to the No–Show and Twin Paradoxes.

6.1.8.1 Example

Suppose there are 19 voters who must elect one out of four candidates, *a, b, c, d* and whose preference orderings among these candidates are as follows:

No. of voters	Preference orderings
5	$d \succ b \succ c \succ a$
4	$b \succ c \succ a \succ d$
3	$a \succ d \succ c \succ b$
3	$a \succ d \succ b \succ c$
4	$c \succ a \succ b \succ d$

These preference orderings can be depicted as the following paired comparisons matrix:

	a	*b*	*c*	*d*
a	–	10	6	14
b	9	–	12	8
c	13	7	–	8
d	5	11	11	–

Here the social preference ordering is cyclical ($c \succ a \succ d \succ b \succ c$). So according to the Minimax procedure one should elect that candidate whose worst loss is smallest. From the paired comparisons matrix it is seen that the worst loss of candidates *a, b, c, d,* is 13, 11, 12, and 14, respectively, so candidate *b* is elected.

Now suppose that, *ceteris paribus*, three of the four voters with preference ordering $c \succ a \succ b \succ d$ decide not to participate in the election. In this case the paired comparisons matrix changes as follows:

	a	*b*	*c*	*d*
a	–	7	6	11
b	9	–	12	5
c	10	4	–	5
d	5	11	11	–

The social preference ordering is still cyclical but the worst losses of the four candidates are now 10, 11, 12, 11 for candidates *a, b, c, d,* respectively, so according to the Minimax procedure candidate *a* is elected—which is preferable from the point of view of the absent voters—thereby demonstrating the vulnerability of the Minimax procedure to the No–Show Paradox.

We also have here an instance of the Twin Paradox. We have just seen that if, *ceteris paribus*, only one of the four voters whose preference orderings are $c \succ a \succ b \succ d$ participates in the election then according to the Minimax procedure candidate *a* is elected. But if this voter's three clone brothers join the electorate then, as we have seen at the beginning of Example 6.1.8.1, candidate *b* is elected according to the Minimax procedure—thereby demonstrating this procedure's vulnerability to the Twin Paradox.

6.1.9 *Truncation Paradox*

Example 6.1.9.1 demonstrates the vulnerability of the Minimax procedure to the Truncation Paradox.

6.1.9.1 Example

As we have seen in the first part of Example 6.1.8.1, candidate *b* would be elected under the Minimax procedure. Now suppose that, *ceteris paribus*, the four voters whose preference ordering is $c \succ a \succ b \succ d$ would decide to state only their top two preferences, *c* and *a*. This would lead to the assumption that the probability that these voters prefer *b* to *d* is equal to the probability that they prefer *d* to *b*, which would result, in turn, in the following paired comparisons matrix:

	a	*b*	*c*	*d*
a	–	10	6	14
b	9	–	12	6
c	13	7	–	8
d	5	13	11	–

From this paired comparisons matrix it is easy to see that candidate *c*'s largest loss (12 against candidate *b*) is smallest, hence this candidate will be elected under the Minimax procedure—which is certainly preferable for the voters whose top preference is *c*—thus demonstrating the vulnerability of the Minimax procedure to the Truncation Paradox.

6.2 The (In)Vulnerability of Dodgson's Procedure to Various Paradoxes

6.2.1 Condorcet Winner Paradox

Dodgson's method chooses the candidate that can be made the Condorcet Winner with a minimum number of binary preference switches. Obviously, the Condorcet Winner needs no such switches at all while all other alternatives require some preference inversions to become a Condorcet Winner. Hence the Condorcet Winner is, *ipso facto*, the Dodgson winner.

6.2.2 Absolute Majority Winner Paradox

Since the Absolute Majority Winner is a special case of a Condorcet Winner, it follows from the argument above that Dodgson's procedure elects the Absolute Majority Winner whenever one exists.

6.2.3 *Pareto-Dominated Candidate Paradox*

Pareto-dominated candidate, say x, cannot be elected by Dodgson's procedure since the dominating candidate, say y, needs strictly fewer binary preference switches to become the Condorcet Winner. This is because y defeats in pairwise comparisons by a majority of votes all those candidates that x beats and, in addition, it defeats x.

6.2.4 *The Condorcet Loser and Preference Inversion Paradoxes*

Example 6.2.4.1 demonstrates the vulnerability of Dodgson's procedure to the Condorcet Loser Paradox.

6.2.4.1 Example

This example is due to Fishburn (1977, p. 477). Suppose there are seven voters whose preference orderings among eight candidates, *a*, *b*, *c*, *d*, *e*, *f*, *g*, *x*, are as follows:

No. of voters	Preference orderings
1	$a \succ b \succ c \succ d \succ x \succ e \succ f \succ g$
1	$g \succ a \succ b \succ c \succ x \succ d \succ e \succ f$
1	$f \succ g \succ a \succ b \succ x \succ c \succ d \succ e$
1	$e \succ f \succ g \succ a \succ x \succ b \succ c \succ d$
1	$d \succ e \succ f \succ g \succ x \succ a \succ b \succ c$
1	$c \succ d \succ e \succ f \succ x \succ g \succ a \succ b$
1	$b \succ c \succ d \succ e \succ x \succ f \succ g \succ a$

The social preference ordering contains a top cycle $[a \succ b \succ c \succ d \succ e \succ f \succ g \succ a] \succ x$. It can be presented by the following paired comparisons matrix:

	a	*b*	*c*	*d*	*e*	*f*	*g*	*x*
a	–	6	5	4	3	2	1	4
b	1	–	6	5	4	3	2	4
c	2	1	–	6	5	4	3	4
d	3	2	1	–	6	5	4	4
e	4	3	2	1	–	6	5	4
f	5	4	3	2	1	–	6	4
g	6	5	4	3	2	1	–	4
x	3	3	3	3	3	3	3	–

As can easily be seen from this matrix, candidate x is a Condorcet Loser as this candidate is beaten in pairwise comparisons by each of the other seven candidates. Nevertheless, candidate x will be elected in this case by Dodgson's procedure because for x to become a Condorcet Winner only four preference inversions are needed (e.g., it is sufficient for any of the voters to move candidate x from 5th to 1st place in his/her preference ordering), whereas for any of the other candidates to become a Condorcet Winner at least six preference inversions are needed.

This example can also be used to demonstrate the vulnerability of Dodgson's procedure to the Preference Inversion Paradox. If all voters invert their preference orderings in this example then x becomes a Condorcet Winner and hence is elected under Dodgson's procedure.

6.2.5 *The Absolute Majority Loser Paradox*

Example 6.2.5.1 demonstrates the vulnerability of Dodgson's procedure to the Absolute Majority Loser Paradox. Example 6.1.2.1 can also be used to demonstrate this paradox.

6.2.5.1 Example

Suppose there are 31 voters whose preference orderings among four candidates, w, x,y, and z are as follows:

No. of voters	Preference orderings
10	$x \succ y \succ z \succ w$
6	$z \succ x \succ y \succ w$
5	$w \succ z \succ x \succ y$
10	$w \succ y \succ z \succ x$

The social preference ordering contains a top cycle $[x \succ y \succ z \succ x] \succ w$. It can be presented by the following paired comparisons matrix:

	w	x	y	z
w	–	15	15	15
x	16	–	21	10
y	16	10	–	20
z	16	21	11	–

As can easily be seen from this matrix, w is an Absolute Majority Loser as this candidate constitutes the bottom preference of an absolute majority (16) of the voters. Nevertheless, candidate w is elected in this example according to Dodgson's procedure because the number of preference inversions s/he needs to become a Condorcet Winner (3) is smaller than that needed by candidates *x*,*y*, and *z* (who need 6,6, and 5 preference inversions, respectively, to become Condorcet Winners) —thereby demonstrating the vulnerability of Dodgson's procedure to the Absolute Majority Loser Paradox.

6.2.6 *Lack of Monotonicity, No-Show, Twin and SCC Paradoxes*

Example 6.2.6.1 demonstrates the vulnerability of Dodgson's procedure to lack of monotonicity, No–Show Paradox, Twin Paradox and SCC Paradox. At least four candidates must exist for this to occur (Fishburn 1982, p. 132)

6.2.6.1 Example

This example was adapted from Fishburn (1977, p. 478). Suppose there are 100 voters who are divided into four groups, who must elect one out of five candidates *a, b, c, d, e,* under Dodgson's procedure, and whose preference orderings among the candidates are as follows:

Group	No. of voters	Preference orderings
G1	42	$b \succ a \succ c \succ d \succ e$
G2	26	$a \succ e \succ c \succ d \succ b$
G3	21	$e \succ d \succ b \succ a \succ c$
G4	11	$e \succ a \succ b \succ d \succ c$

The social preference ordering has a top cycle: $[b \succ a \succ e \succ b] \succ c \succ d$. It can be depicted as the following paired comparisons matrix:

	a	*b*	*c*	*d*	*e*
a	–	37	100	79	68
b	63	–	74	53	42
c	0	26	–	68	42
d	21	47	32	–	42
e	32	58	58	58	–

For candidate *a* to become the Condorcet Winner at least 14 voters in group G1 must change $b \succ a$ in their preference ordering to $a \succ b$, i.e., a total of 14 changes.

For candidate *b* to become the Condorcet Winner at least 9 voters from group G4 must first change $a \succ b$ to $b \succ a$ and thereafter $e \succ b$ to $b \succ e$ in their preference ordering, i.e., a total of 18 changes.

For candidate e to become the Condorcet Winner at least 19 voters in group G2 must change $a \succ e$ in their preference ordering to $e \succ a$, i.e., a total of 19 changes.

Candidates c and d require more than 50 binary preference switches each to become the Condorcet Winner.

Since the number of changes needed in the voters' preference orderings in order for a to become the Condorcet Winner is the smallest, a would be elected under Dodgson's procedure.

Now suppose that, *ceteris paribus*, the 11 voters in group G4 *increase* their support of candidate a by changing their preference orderings from $e \succ a \succ b \succ d \succ c$ to $a \succ e \succ b \succ d \succ c$. This change can be depicted by the following paired comparisons matrix:

	a	b	c	d	e
a	–	37	100	79	79
b	63	–	74	53	42
c	0	26	–	68	42
d	21	47	32	–	42
e	21	58	58	58	–

From this matrix it is possible to see that despite the increase in a's support it would still take at least 14 persons from group G1 to change in their preference orderings $b \succ a$ to $a \succ b$ in order for a to become the Condorcet Winner, whereas now for b to become the Condorcet Winner only 9 voters in modified G4 would have to change $e \succ b$ to $b \succ e$ in their preference orderings. So since the number of changes needed for b to become the Condorcet Winner is smallest, b would be elected under Dodgson's procedure—thereby demonstrating lack of monotonicity.[2]

The first part of Example 6.2.6.1 can also be used to demonstrate the vulnerability of Dodgson's procedure to the No–Show and Twin Paradoxes. If 20 of the 21 voters in group G3 decide not to participate in the election then b becomes the Condorcet Winner and will be elected according to Dodgson's procedure. The

[2]Note that by increasing a's support the 11 voters of group G4 obtained the election of b which for them is a less preferable alternative than the election of a. In demonstrating the non-monotonicity paradox under the other four procedures surveyed in this book that are susceptible to this paradox (Plurality with Runoff, Alternative Vote, Coombs, Nanson), it is exemplified not only that an original winner, w, loses after one or more voters, V_i, increase their support of w by moving w upwards in their preference ordering, but also that the voters belonging to V_i *benefit* from this because the new winner, y, is ranked higher than w in V_i's original preference ordering. However, under Dodgson's procedure it is impossible to construct such an example because when w rises in V_i's ranking, the indirect benefit, if any, goes to the candidates ranked below w in V_i's preference ordering who now find the candidates who had been ranked above w more accessible. But if V_i's initial ranking is assumed to be sincere, then it follows, by definition, that the members of V_i prefer w over any of the candidates ranked below w. So if some candidate ranked below w is elected then the members of V_i are harmed. Hence non-monotonicity under Dodgson's procedure cannot arise from strategic voting. The first-named author is grateful to Nicolaus Tideman for this insight (private communication 3.8.2011).

election of b is of course preferred by the members of group G3 over the election of a thus demonstrating the vulnerability of Dodgson's procedure to the No–Show Paradox. Adding those 20 clones back to retrieve the original profile shows that Dodgson's procedure is also vulnerable to the Twin Paradox.

Example 6.2.6.1 can also be used to demonstrate the vulnerability of Dodgson's procedure to the SCC Paradox. As we have seen in the first part of Example 6.2.6.1 candidate a is selected by Dodgson's procedure. However if, *ceteris paribus*, candidate e drops out of the race then candidate b becomes the Condorcet Winner and is elected by Dodgson's procedure—in violation of SCC.

6.2.7 *Reinforcement*

Example 6.2.7.1 demonstrates the vulnerability of Dodgson's procedure to the Reinforcement Paradox.

6.2.7.1 Example

This example is due to Fishburn (1977, p. 484). Suppose there are two districts, I and II, in each of them one of four candidates, w,x,y,z, must be elected.

In district I there are seven voters, four with preference ordering $x \succ y \succ z \succ w$ and three with preference ordering $y \succ x \succ z \succ w$. Since x is here the Condorcet Winner, x is elected according to Dodgson's procedure.

In district II there are 12 voters whose preference orderings are as follows:

No. of voters	Preference orderings
1	$x \succ y \succ z \succ w$
2	$y \succ x \succ z \succ w$
3	$w \succ y \succ x \succ z$
3	$z \succ w \succ y \succ x$
3	$x \succ z \succ w \succ y$

These orderings can be presented as the following paired comparisons matrix:

	w	x	y	z
w	–	6	9	3
x	6	–	4	9
y	3	8	–	6
z	9	3	6	–

Here the social preference ordering is cyclical [$w \succ y \succ x \succ z \succ w$]. For x to become the Condorcet Winner only four preference inversions are needed (the two voters whose top preference is y should change their top preference to x, and one of the three voters whose top preference is w should change his/her top preference to x), whereas for any of the other candidates to become a Condorcet Winner more than four preference inversions are needed. So according to Dodgson's procedure candidate x is elected also in district II.

Now suppose that, *ceteris paribus*, the two districts are amalgamated into a single district with 19 voters. In this case candidate y becomes the Condorcet Winner and is elected according to Dodgson's procedure—thereby demonstrating its vulnerability to the Reinforcement Paradox.

6.2.8 *Truncation Paradox*

Example 6.2.8.1 demonstrates Dodgson's vulnerability to the Truncation Paradox.

6.2.8.1 Example

Suppose there are 49 voters whose preference orderings among five candidates, *a, b, c, d, e* are as follows:

No. of voters	Preference orderings
11	$b \succ a \succ d \succ e \succ c$
10	$e \succ c \succ b \succ d \succ a$
10	$a \succ c \succ d \succ b \succ e$
2	$e \succ c \succ d \succ b \succ a$
2	$e \succ d \succ c \succ b \succ a$
2	$c \succ b \succ a \succ d \succ e$
1	$d \succ c \succ b \succ a \succ e$
1	$a \succ b \succ d \succ e \succ c$
10	$e \succ d \succ a \succ b \succ c$

These orderings can be presented as the following paired comparisons matrix:

	a	*b*	*c*	*d*	*e*
a	–	21	32	24	25
b	28	–	22	24	25
c	17	27	–	24	13
d	25	25	25	–	25
e	24	24	36	24	–

Here candidate d is the Condorcet Winner so this candidate is elected according to Dodgson's procedure. However, if the 10 voters whose preference ordering is $e \succ d \succ a \succ b \succ c$ decide to reveal only their top preference (e)—in which case one assumes that these voters prefer candidate e over all the other four candidates and that all possible preference orderings among these candidates are equiprobable—then one obtains the following paired comparisons matrix:

	a	b	c	d	e
a	–	16	27	29	25
b	33	–	17	29	25
c	22	32	–	29	13
d	20	20	20	–	25
e	24	24	36	24	–

From this matrix we see that the social preference ordering is cyclical ($d \succ e \succ c \succ b \succ a \succ d$). So, according to Dodgson's procedure candidate e is elected in this situation because for candidate e to become a Condorcet Winner only three preference inversions are needed (if one of the 11 $b \succ a \succ d \succ e \succ c$ voters will change his/her preference ordering to $e \succ b \succ a \succ d \succ c$), whereas for any of the other candidates to become a Condorcet Winner more than three preference inversions are needed—thereby demonstrating the vulnerability of Dodgson's procedure to the Truncation Paradox.

6.3 The (In)Vulnerability of Nanson's Procedure to Various Paradoxes

6.3.1 *Condorcet Winner Paradox*

The Condorcet Winner, if one exists, is elected by Nanson's method. In fact, that was the main goal of its designer E. J. Nanson. The elimination criterion guarantees that only candidates with strictly higher than average Borda scores survive each stage of computation. It can be seen that the Condorcet Winner never has an average or smaller than average Borda score. This is because in the pairwise comparison matrix all entries on the row corresponding to the Condorcet Winner are strictly greater than $v/2$ (where v is the number of voters). Hence the Borda score of the Condorcet Winner is strictly greater than $v(n - 1)/2$. Now, as the sum of the Borda scores of all candidates in an n–candidate race is $vn(n - 1)/2$ (where n is the number of candidates), the average Borda score is $v(n - 1)/2$, i.e., strictly less than the score of the Condorcet Winner. Hence, the Condorcet Winner survives the elimination process of Nanson's method and is elected.

6.3.2 Absolute Majority Paradox

Absolute Majority Winner is a special case of the Condorcet Winner and will thus be elected by Nanson's method in virtue of the argument above.

6.3.3 Condorcet Loser Paradox

Condorcet Loser necessarily receives a strictly smaller than average Borda score and will thus be eliminated by Nanson's method. The Borda score of a Condorcet Loser is strictly less than $v(n-1)/2$ which is the average Borda score in any n-candidate contest. Hence the Condorcet Loser will be eliminated at the outset and, thus, cannot be elected by Nanson's method.

6.3.4 Absolute Majority Loser Paradox

Absolute Majority Loser is a special case of the Condorcet Loser and hence cannot be elected by Nanson's method in virtue of the above argument.

6.3.5 Pareto-Dominated Candidate Paradox

If x is Pareto-dominated by y, then the latter's Borda score will be strictly larger than the former's. Hence, if y is eliminated, so is x, but not vice versa. If both survive after the last elimination round, y will defeat x, but in any event x will not be elected.

6.3.6 Preference Inversion Paradox

Since all entries of the original pairwise comparison matrix are inverted in the matrix corresponding to the inverted profile, the Borda scores will also yield an inverted order of the candidates. Thus, preference inversion is averted (see Saari and Barney 2003, p. 28).

6.3.7 Lack of Monotonicity Paradox

Example 6.3.7.1 demonstrates the vulnerability of Nanson's procedure to lack of monotonicity.

6.3.7.1 Example

Suppose there are 100 voters who are to elect one out of four candidates *a, b, c, d* under Nanson's procedure. The preference orderings of the voters are as follows:

No. of voters	Preference orderings
30	$c \succ a \succ d \succ b$
21	$b \succ d \succ c \succ a$
20	$a \succ b \succ d \succ c$
12	$b \succ a \succ c \succ d$
12	$a \succ c \succ b \succ d$
5	$a \succ c \succ d \succ b$

The Borda scores of the candidates *a, b, c* and *d* are 195, 151, 157 and 97, respectively. Since the average score is 150, *d* is eliminated. The recomputed Borda scores for the remaining candidates *a, b* and *c* are 116, 86 and 98, with the average of 100. Only *a* survives the second round of computing and is thus the winner.

Suppose now that the 12 voters with $b \succ a \succ c \succ d$ ranking would improve the winner *a*'s position by changing their preference orderings to $a \succ b \succ c \succ d$. The ensuing Borda scores are now 207, 139, 157 and 97 for *a, b, c,* and *d*, respectively. Hence *b* and *d* are eliminated whereupon *c* wins. Thus Nanson's procedure is non–monotonic.

6.3.8 Reinforcement Paradox

Example 6.2.7.1, which demonstrates the vulnerability of Dodgson's procedure to the Reinforcement Paradox, can also be used to demonstrate the vulnerability of Nanson's procedure to this paradox.

6.3.9 Truncation Paradox

Example 6.3.9.1 demonstrates the vulnerability of Nanson's procedure to the Truncation Paradox.

6.3.9.1 Example

Suppose there are 43 voters divided into six groups whose preference orderings among four candidates *a, b, c, d* are as follows:

Group	No. of voters	Preference orderings
G1	9	$a \succ b \succ d \succ c$
G2	5	$a \succ c \succ b \succ d$
G3	2	$a \succ c \succ d \succ b$
G4	5	$b \succ a \succ c \succ d$
G5	9	$b \succ d \succ c \succ a$
G6	13	$c \succ b \succ a \succ d$

Given the above preference orderings, the number of points awarded to candidates *a, b, c,* and *d* in the first counting round are 71, 91, 67, and 29, respectively. Since the average number of points is 64.5, candidate *d* is deleted and a second counting round is conducted. The number of points awarded to candidates *a, b, c* in this round is 37, 50, and 42, respectively. As the average number of points in this round is 43, both candidates *a* and *c* are eliminated so candidate *b* is elected.

Suppose now that, *ceteris paribus*, all voters belonging to groups G2 and G6 (who are not very happy with the prospect that candidate *b* will be elected) decide not to rank (i.e., truncate) candidate *b* in their ballots. In this case we apply to the truncated ballots the revised Borda Truncated scoring system proposed by Fishburn (1974, p. 543) and mentioned in Example 5.1.9.1 (Chap. 5). As a result we obtain that the number of points awarded to candidates *a, b, c, d* are 84, 60, 67, and 47, respectively. As the average number of points in this case is also 64.5, candidates *b* and *d* are eliminated and a second counting round is conducted. The number of points awarded to candidates *a* and *c* in this round is 21 and 22, respectively, so candidate *c* is elected. This result is of course preferred by the voters of groups G2 and G6 to the election of candidate *b*, thereby demonstrating the susceptibility of Nanson's procedure to the Truncation Paradox.

6.3.10 No–Show and Twin Paradoxes

Example 6.3.10.1 demonstrates the vulnerability of Nanson's procedure to the No–Show and Twin Paradoxes.

6.3.10.1 Example

Suppose there are 19 voters whose preference orderings among four candidates, *a, b, c, d*, are as follows:

No. of voters	Preference orderings
5	$a \succ b \succ d \succ c$
5	$b \succ c \succ d \succ a$

(continued)

(continued)

No. of voters	Preference orderings
6	$c \succ a \succ d \succ b$
1	$c \succ b \succ a \succ d$
2	$c \succ b \succ d \succ a$

Here the Borda scores of candidates *a, b, c, d* are 28, 31, 37, 18, respectively, and the average Borda score is 28.5. Therefore candidates *a* and *d* are eliminated, whereupon candidate *b* is elected under Nanson's procedure. But if, *ceteris paribus*, one of the two last voters abstains then candidate *c*—the abstainer's most preferred candidate—is elected under Nanson's procedure, thus demonstrating the vulnerability of this procedure to the No–Show Paradox.

We also have here an instance of the Twin Paradox: we have just seen that if there is only one voter with preference ordering $c \succ b \succ d \succ a$ then, *ceteris paribus*, candidate *c* will be elected under Nanson's procedure. But if s/he is joined by a twin with the same preference ordering then *b* will be elected under Nanson's procedure, thus demonstrating the vulnerability of this procedure to the Twin Paradox.

6.3.11 *SCC Paradox*

Example 6.3.11.1 demonstrates the vulnerability of Nanson's procedure to the SCC Paradox.

6.3.11.1 Example

This example is due to Fishburn (1977, p. 486). Suppose there are 86 voters who must elect one out of four candidates, *a, b, c,* or *d*, under Nanson's procedure and whose preference orderings are as follows:

No. of voters	Preference orderings
20	$d \succ a \succ b \succ c$
20	$d \succ b \succ c \succ a$
12	$c \succ b \succ d \succ a$
28	$a \succ c \succ b \succ d$
3	$b \succ c \succ a \succ d$
3	$c \succ b \succ a \succ d$

Accordingly, the number of Borda points awarded to candidates *a*, *b*, *c*, and *d* are 130, 127, 127, and 132, respectively—so candidates *b, c* are deleted and in the second counting round candidate *d* gets more Borda points (52) than candidate *a* (34) and hence *d* is elected.

Now suppose that, *ceteris paribus*, candidate *a* drops out of the race. In this case the number of Borda points awarded to candidates *b,c* and *d* are 89, 89, and 80, respectively, so there is a tie (to be broken randomly) between *b* and *c*—in violation of SCC.

6.4 The (In)Vulnerability of Copeland's Procedure to Various Paradoxes

6.4.1 Condorcet Winner Paradox

Let *Cop(x)* be the Copeland score of candidate *x*, i.e., the number of other candidates *x* defeats in pairwise comparisons by a majority of votes. If *y* is the Condorcet Winner its *Cop(y)*, by definition, is $n - 1$ (where n is the number of candidates) since it beats all other candidates. No other candidate can have as high a Copeland score as *y*'s because they are all defeated by *y* and consequently have strictly smaller Copeland scores than *y*. Thus the Condorcet Winner is elected by Copeland's procedure.

6.4.2 Absolute Majority Winner Paradox

The Absolute Majority Winner is a special case of the Condorcet Winner and, hence, the argument above applies to show that Absolute Majority Winners are always elected by Copeland's procedure.

6.4.3 Condorcet Loser Paradox

A Condorcet Loser gets the Copeland score of 0 since it defeats no other candidate. All other alternatives get the Copeland score of at least 1 by virtue of beating the Condorcet Loser. Hence, the Copeland procedure never elects a Condorcet Loser.

6.4.4 Absolute Majority Loser Paradox

Absolute Majority Loser is a special case of the Condorcet Loser and thus the argument above applies to show that Copeland's procedure does not elect the Absolute Majority Loser.

6.4.5 *Pareto-Dominated Candidate Paradox*

If x Pareto-dominates y, then x beats all candidates that y beats as well as y itself. Hence its Copeland score is strictly larger than y's. Thus the latter is not elected.

6.4.6 *Lack of Monotonicity Paradox*

Copeland's procedure is monotonic under fixed electorate. This is so because if candidate x is the Copeland winner and then its position is improved, *ceteris paribus,* it still defeats the candidates it defeated at the outset and possibly some others. So, its score is at least as large as originally. No other candidate beats more candidates than previously as a result of the improvement of x's position. Some of them may lose to x, however. Hence, the other candidates at best maintain their original Copeland scores, while x's score is at least equal to the original (winning) one. Thus, x remains the winner. However, in variable electorates Copeland's procedure is vulnerable to monotonicity failure. For examples see Felsenthal and Nurmi (2016, 2017).

6.4.7 *Preference Inversion Paradox*

Let x be the Copeland winner in a profile. Upon reversal of the profile, all victories of x are turned into defeats and, hence, some of the previous Copeland non-winners may become a Copeland winner in the inverted profile. Hence, Copeland's method is invulnerable to the Preference Inversion Paradox.

6.4.8 *No–Show, Twin and Truncation Paradoxes*

Example 6.4.8.1 demonstrates the vulnerability of Copeland's procedure to the No–Show, Twin, and Truncation paradoxes.

6.4.8.1 Example

Suppose there are 33 voters who must select one out of four candidates, a, b, c, or d, and whose preference orderings among these four candidates are as follows:

No. of voters	Preference orderings
11	$a \succ b \succ c \succ d$
2	$b \succ c \succ a \succ d$

(continued)

(continued)

No. of voters	Preference orderings
12	$b \succ c \succ d \succ a$
4	$c \succ a \succ d \succ b$
2	$d \succ a \succ b \succ c$
2	$d \succ b \succ a \succ c$

This preference list can be depicted as the following paired comparisons matrix:

	a	*b*	*c*	*d*
a	–	17	15	17
b	16	–	29	25
c	18	4	–	29
d	16	8	4	–

From this paired comparisons matrix we see that the social preference ordering has a top cycle $[a \succ b \succ c \succ a] \succ d$, so according to Copeland's procedure there is a tie between *a*, *b* and *c*.

Now suppose that, *ceteris paribus*, one of the two voters whose preference ordering is $b \succ c \succ a \succ d$ decides not to participate in the election. This change will result in the following paired comparisons matrix:

	a	*b*	*c*	*d*
a	–	17	15	16
b	15	–	28	24
c	17	4	–	28
d	16	8	4	–

From this matrix we can see that according to Copeland's procedure each of candidates *b* and *c* gets two Copeland points (since each of these two candidates beats two other candidates), while candidates *a* and *d* get 1.5 and 0.5 points, respectively. This result is certainly preferable from the point of view of the voter who decided not to participate, thus demonstrating the vulnerability of the Copeland's procedure to the No–Show Paradox.

The same example can also be used to demonstrate the vulnerability of Copeland's procedure to the Twin Paradox. We have just seen that in the second part of this example one obtains a tie between candidates *b* and *c*. So one could expect, presumably, that if a twin brother of the voter with preference ordering $b \succ c \succ a \succ d$ joins the electorate (instead of abstaining), the chances of candidate *b* to get elected would increase. But as we have seen from the first part of this example when, *ceteris paribus*, two voters with preference ordering $b \succ c \succ a \succ d$ exist in the electorate, then the chances of candidate *b* to get elected according to Copeland's procedure *decrease* because in this case one obtains a tie between *b* and two other candidates (*a* and *c*), whereas one obtains a tie between *b* and just one other candidate (c) when only one voter with preference ordering $b \succ c \succ a \succ d$ exists in the electorate—thus demonstrating the vulnerability of Copeland's procedure to the Twin Paradox.

To demonstrate the Truncation Paradox suppose that, *ceteris paribus*, in the first part of Example 6.4.8.1 the two voters with preference ordering $b \succ c \succ a \succ d$ would decide to reveal only their top preference. In this case one would have to assume that all the six possible preference orderings of these voters among candidates a, c, d are equiprobable (or, equivalently, that they are indifferent among them) and, consequently, one would obtain the following paired comparisons matrix:

	a	b	c	d
a	–	17	16	16
b	16	–	29	25
c	17	4	–	28
d	17	8	5	–

From this paired comparisons matrix it is easy to see that according to Copeland's procedure there would be a tie between candidates b and c (each obtaining two points)—which is a preferable result from the point of view of the two $b \succ c \succ a \succ d$ voters over a tie among candidates a, b, c which was obtained, *ceteris paribus*, when these voters revealed their entire preference ordering among all four candidates.

6.4.9 Reinforcement Paradox

Example 6.4.9.1 demonstrates the vulnerability of Copeland's procedure to the Reinforcement Paradox.

6.4.9.1 Example

Suppose there are two districts, I and II. In district I there are three voters whose preference orderings among four candidates, a, b, c, and d, are as follows:

No. of voters	Preference orderings
1	$a \succ b \succ c \succ d$
1	$b \succ d \succ c \succ a$
1	$d \succ c \succ a \succ b$

and in district II there are two voters, one with preference ordering $b \succ d \succ c \succ a$, and the other with preference ordering $d \succ b \succ c \succ a$.

According to Copeland's procedure there is a tie between candidates b and d in each of the two districts.

However, *ceteris paribus*, if the two districts are amalgamated into a single district of five voters then one obtains the following preference list:

No. of voters	Preference orderings
1	$a \succ b \succ c \succ d$
2	$b \succ d \succ c \succ a$
1	$d \succ b \succ c \succ a$
1	$d \succ c \succ a \succ b$

This preference list can be depicted as the following paired comparisons matrix:

	a	b	c	d
a	–	2	1	1
b	3	–	4	3
c	4	1	–	1
d	4	2	4	–

From this paired comparisons matrix it is clear that candidate b is the Condorcet Winner and hence is elected according to Copeland's procedure—contrary to the Reinforcement axiom.

6.4.10 SCC Paradox

Example 6.1.3.1 can be used to demonstrate the vulnerability of Copeland's procedure to the SCC Paradox. According to that example there is a tie according to Copeland's procedure between candidates a and d. However if, *ceteris paribus*, candidate b is eliminated then candidate a becomes the Condorcet Winner and is elected by Copeland's procedure—in violation of the SCC postulate.

6.5 The (In)Vulnerability of Black's Procedure to Various Paradoxes

6.5.1 Condorcet Winner Paradox

Black's procedure elects, by definition, the Condorcet Winner when one exists. Hence, it is invulnerable to the Condorcet Winner Paradox.

6.5.2 Absolute Majority Winner Paradox

Black's procedure avoids the Absolute Majority Winner Paradox by virtue of the fact that the Absolute Majority Winner is a special case of the Condorcet Winner. Therefore, the above argument applies.

6.5.3 Condorcet Loser Paradox

Black's procedure cannot elect a Condorcet Loser since if there is a Condorcet Winner, it cannot be the Condorcet Loser, and if there is no Condorcet Winner, the Borda winner wins. The latter, in turn, cannot be the Condorcet Loser as we saw in the preceding (Cf. Sect. 5.1.2 in Chap. 5).

6.5.4 Absolute Majority Loser Paradox

Absolute Majority Loser is neither the Condorcet Winner nor the Borda winner. Hence it cannot be elected by Black's procedure.

6.5.5 Pareto-Dominated Candidate Paradox

If x is Pareto-dominated by y, then x is not the Condorcet Winner (since it is beaten by at least y). Nor can x be the Borda winner, since y's Borda score is strictly larger than x's. Therefore, the Pareto-dominated candidate cannot be elected by Black's procedure.

6.5.6 Lack of Monotonicity Paradox

If x is the Black winner it is because it is either the Condorcet or Borda winner (or both). An improvement of x's position *vis–à–vis* some candidates, *ceteris paribus*, will maintain its status as the Condorcet Winner (if it was one at the outset) since no other candidate beats more others than it did at the outset, while x defeats at least as many others as at the outset. An improvement of the kind just described will increase x's Borda score, but all other scores either remain the same or diminish. Hence, Black's procedure is monotonic in fixed electorates. In variable electorates, on the other hand, Black's procedure is vulnerable to monotonicity failure. For examples see Felsenthal and Nurmi (2016, 2017).

6.5.7 *Preference Inversion Paradox*

It is obvious that the Preference Inversion Paradox cannot happen under Black's procedure if there is no Condorcet Winner in both the original and inverted profile since in these cases the Borda winner is the Black outcome. Indeed, Saari and Barney (2003) have proven that the Borda count is the only positional procedure that is invulnerable to Preference Inversion Paradox. If a Condorcet Winner, say x, exists in the original profile, but not in the inverted one, the Borda scores determine the Black winner in the latter. By inversion x is now defeated by all other candidates in pairwise comparison and is thus the Condorcet Loser. This means that its Borda score is strictly less than the average Borda score in the inverted profile. Hence, there must be a candidate with a strictly higher Borda score than x, whereby x is not elected. If, on the other hand, there is no Condorcet Winner at the outset, the Borda winner, say y, is elected. Now, after the inversion y is not the Borda winner in the inverted profile. But can it be the Condorcet Winner? No, since its Borda score in the inverted profile is the smallest. The Condorcet Winner can never have the smallest Borda score. Hence, y is not the Black winner in the inverted profile. Thus Black's method avoids the Preference Inversion Paradox.

6.5.8 *No–Show, Twin and Truncation Paradoxes*

Example 6.5.8.1 demonstrates the vulnerability of Black's procedure to the No–Show, Twin, and Truncation paradoxes.

6.5.8.1 Example

Suppose there are 16 voters whose preference orderings among five candidates, a, b, c, d, e, are as follows:

No. of voters	Preference orderings
3	$d \succ e \succ a \succ b \succ c$
3	$e \succ a \succ c \succ b \succ d$
4	$c \succ d \succ e \succ a \succ b$
3	$d \succ e \succ b \succ c \succ a$
3	$e \succ b \succ a \succ d \succ c$

Here d is the Condorcet Winner and hence is elected under Black's procedure. Suppose now that, *ceteris paribus*, two of the voters whose preference ordering is $e \succ b \succ a \succ d \succ c$ decide not to participate in the election. As a result the social preference ordering becomes cyclical ($a \succ b = c = d \succ e \succ a$) and e emerges as the Borda winner and is therefore elected under Black's procedure. Since e is ranked first by the two absent voters, it turns out that they obtained a better outcome by not participating in the election—thereby demonstrating the vulnerability of Black's procedure to the No–Show Paradox.

We also have here an instance of the Twin Paradox: if, *ceteris paribus*, the two absent voters decide to participate in the election and join their clone brother, then d becomes the Condorcet Winner and will be elected under Black's procedure—thereby demonstrating the vulnerability of Black's procedure to the Twin Paradox.

Obviously, not voting at all is an extreme version of Truncation and hence the above example can also be used to show that Black's procedure is vulnerable to the Truncation Paradox. Thus if, *ceteris paribus*, all three voters whose preference ordering is $e \succ b \succ a \succ d \succ c$ truncate their preference ordering after a, i.e., if they do not express their preferences between c and d—which would automatically be considered to mean that they prefer each of the three ranked alternatives over c and d and are indifferent between c and d—then the social preference ordering will become cyclic ($d \succ e \succ a \succ b \succ c \succ d$) and e will emerge as the Borda winner to be elected under Black's procedure—which is a preferable outcome for these voters.

The vulnerability of Borda's procedure (and hence also Black's) to the Truncation Paradox when a Condorcet Winner does not exist initially is demonstrated in Example 5.1.9.1 (Chap. 5).

6.5.9 *Reinforcement Paradox*

Example 6.5.9.1 demonstrates the vulnerability of Black's procedure to the Reinforcement Paradox.

6.5.9.1 Example

Suppose there are two districts, I and II. In district I there are 5 voters whose preference orderings among three candidates, a, b, and c, are as follows:

No. of voters	Preference orderings
2	$a \succ b \succ c$
2	$b \succ c \succ a$
1	$c \succ a \succ b$

and in District II there are 9 voters whose preference ordering among these three candidates are as follows:

No. of voters	Preference orderings
5	$b \succ c \succ a$
4	$c \succ a \succ b$

The social preference ordering in district I is cyclical ($a \succ b \succ c \succ a$), so according to Borda's (and Black's) procedure candidate b, whose Borda score (6) is largest, is elected in this district. In district II candidate b is the Condorcet Winner, so according to Black's procedure b is elected in this district too.

Now suppose that, *ceteris paribus*, the two districts are amalgamated into a single large district of 14 voters whose preference ordering among the three candidates are as follows:

No. of voters	Preference orderings
2	$a \succ b \succ c$
7	$b \succ c \succ a$
5	$c \succ a \succ b$

As the social preference ordering in the amalgamated district is cyclical ($c \succ a = b \succ c$) candidate c is elected in this district because his/her Borda score (17) is largest—thus demonstrating the vulnerability of Black's procedure to the Reinforcement Paradox.

6.5.10 SCC Paradox

The vulnerability of Black's procedure to SCC is demonstrated in Example 5.1.9.1 (Chap. 5). When all four candidates compete the social preference ordering has a top cycle [($a \succ b \succ c \succ a$) $\succ d$] so according to Black's procedure candidate c is elected because this candidate has the highest Borda score (13). But if, *ceteris paribus*, candidate a drops out of the race then candidate b becomes the Condorcet Winner and is therefore elected according to Black's procedure—contrary to SCC.

6.5.11 Smith's Condorcet Principle

Example 6.5.11.1 demonstrates the violation of Smith's (1973) Condorcet Principle by Black's procedure.

6.5.11.1 Example

This example is due to Fishburn (1977, p. 480). Suppose there are five voters whose preference orderings among eight candidates a, b, c, d, e, x, y, z, are as follows:

No. of voters	Preference orderings
1	$a \succ b \succ c \succ x \succ y \succ z \succ d \succ e$
1	$e \succ a \succ b \succ x \succ y \succ z \succ c \succ d$
1	$d \succ e \succ a \succ x \succ y \succ z \succ b \succ c$

(continued)

(continued)

No. of voters	Preference orderings
1	$c \succ d \succ e \succ x \succ y \succ z \succ a \succ b$
1	$b \succ c \succ d \succ x \succ y \succ z \succ e \succ a$

These preference orderings can be depicted as the following paired comparisons matrix:

	a	*b*	*c*	*d*	*e*	*x*	*y*	*z*
a	–	4	3	2	1	3	3	3
b	1	–	4	3	2	3	3	3
c	2	1	–	4	3	3	3	3
d	3	2	1	–	4	3	3	3
e	4	3	2	1	–	3	3	3
x	2	2	2	2	2	–	5	5
y	2	2	2	2	2	0	–	5
z	2	2	2	2	2	0	0	–

The social preference ordering here has a top cycle $[a \succ b \succ c \succ d \succ e \succ a] \succ x \succ y \succ z$, so according to Black's procedure one must use Borda's procedure in order to determine which of the eight candidates will be deemed the winner. The Borda count of each of the candidates *a*–*e* is 19, that of candidate *x* is 20, and those of candidates *y* and *z* are 15 and 10, respectively. So according to Black's procedure candidate *x* is elected because s/he has the highest Borda score. However, since Borda's procedure violates here Smith's (1973) Condorcet Principle, so does Black's procedure.[3]

6.6 The (In)Vulnerability of Kemeny's Procedure to Various Paradoxes

6.6.1 *Condorcet Winner Paradox*

The Kemeny ranking has the Condorcet Winner placed first. This was shown by Young and Levenglick (1978). The argument to show this is the following. Take any ranking, say R, of the alternatives that has not the Condorcet Winner, say *x*,

[3]As noted above in Sect. 2.1.3 (cf. Chap. 2), Smith's (1973) Condorcet Principle states that if the set of candidates can be partitioned into two disjoint subsets, *A* and *B*, such that each candidate belonging to *A* can beat in paired comparisons each of the candidates belonging to *B*, then none of the candidates belonging to *B* ought to be elected unless all candidates in *A* are elected. In Example 6.5.11.1 each of candidates *a*–*e* beats in paired comparisons each of the candidates *x,y,z*. However, Borda's procedure (and Black's) elects here candidate *x* although only a single candidate must be elected—in violation of Smith's Condorcet Principle.

ranked first. This cannot be the Kemeny ranking since it is not closest to the observed profile in terms of binary preference switches. To wit, lifting x from its position in R to the top, *ceteris paribus,* thereby forming the ranking R' entails that more voters are in agreement with the pairs involving x in R' than in R, while the number of agreements regarding other pairs of candidates remains the same. Hence the former is closer to the voter preferences than the latter. Thus, the Kemeny ranking has to have x at the top position.

6.6.2 Absolute Majority Winner Paradox

Since the Absolute Majority Winner is also the Condorcet Winner, it will be elected by Kemeny's rule as was shown in the preceding.

6.6.3 Condorcet Loser Paradox

Suppose that y is the Condorcet Loser candidate and that there is a ranking of candidates such that y is at the top of this ranking. This cannot be the Kemeny ranking since reversing the ranking of the top two candidates, say x and y in this ranking, *ceteris paribus,* results in a ranking that is closer to the observed profile than the one where y is at the top.

6.6.4 Absolute Majority Loser Paradox

Absolute Majority Loser is a special kind of Condorcet Loser. Hence, by the argument above it will not be ranked at the top of the Kemeny ranking.

6.6.5 Pareto-Dominated Candidate Paradox

If x Pareto-dominates y, then any ranking with y placed higher than x can be brought closer to the observed profile by switching the order of these two candidates. Hence, y cannot be elected.

6.6.6 Lack of Monotonicity Paradox

Suppose candidate x is at the top of the Kemeny ranking of some profile and then its position is improved, *ceteris paribus,* in some individual preferences. Consequently, some relations involving x are inverted from y to x into x to y for some y. Thus the support of those pairs is stronger than at the outset while no other pairs get more support. Thus, the status of the previous Kemeny winner x is maintained. This holds for fixed electorates. In variable electorates, Kemeny's rule is vulnerable to monotonicity failure. For examples see Felsenthal and Nurmi (2016, 2017).

6.6.7 *Preference Inversion Paradox*

Kemeny's method is invulnerable to preference inversion since the Kemeny ranking of a profile will be inverted upon inverting the profile.

6.6.8 *Reinforcement*

Example 6.6.8.1 demonstrates the vulnerability of Kemeny's procedure to the Reinforcement Paradox. It can also be used to demonstrate the vulnerability of Dodgson's procedure to this paradox.

6.6.8.1 Example

Suppose there are two districts, I and II.

In district I there are two voters whose preference ordering among six candidates are as follows: $x \succ y \succ a \succ b \succ c \succ d$. Here x is the Condorcet Winner and hence will be elected according to Kemeny's procedure.

In district II there are seven voters whose preference ordering among the six candidates are as follows:

No. of voters	Preference orderings
3	$y \succ x \succ a \succ b \succ c \succ d$
1	$a \succ b \succ c \succ d \succ y \succ x$
1	$d \succ a \succ b \succ c \succ y \succ x$
1	$c \succ d \succ a \succ b \succ y \succ x$
1	$x \succ a \succ b \succ c \succ d \succ y$

These preference orderings can be depicted as the following paired comparisons matrix:

	a	b	c	d	x	y
a	–	7	6	5	3	4
b	0	–	6	5	3	4
c	1	1	–	6	3	4
d	2	2	1	–	3	4
x	4	4	4	4	–	1
y	3	3	3	3	6	–

The social preference ordering here is cyclical: x beats each of the four candidates a—d, whereas y beats x but is beaten by each of the four candidates a—d. So it is clear that according to Kemeny's procedure the closest (non-cyclical) social preference ordering here is one in which x is the top–ranked candidate. So in district II too x is elected according to Kemeny's procedure.

However, in the amalgamated district (consisting of districts I and II), we obtain the following paired comparisons matrix:

	a	b	c	d	x	y
a	–	9	8	7	3	4
b	0	–	8	7	3	4
c	1	1	–	8	3	4
d	2	2	1	–	3	4
x	6	6	6	6	–	3
y	5	5	5	5	6	–

According to this matrix y is the Condorcet Winner and hence elected under Kemeny's procedure—thereby demonstrating its vulnerability to the Reinforcement Paradox.

6.6.9 No–Show and Truncation Paradoxes

Example 6.6.9.1 demonstrates the vulnerability of Kemeny's procedure to the No–Show and Truncation Paradoxes.

6.6.9.1 Example

Suppose there are 19 voters whose preference orderings among four candidates, a, b, c, d, are as follows:

No. of voters	Preference orderings
5	$d \succ b \succ c \succ a$
4	$d \succ a \succ b \succ c$
4	$b \succ c \succ a \succ d$
3	$a \succ d \succ c \succ b$
3	$a \succ d \succ b \succ c$

Here a is the Condorcet Winner and is therefore elected under Kemeny's procedure.

Now suppose that, *ceteris paribus*, four of the $d \succ b \succ c \succ a$ voters decide not to participate in the election. As a result we obtain that the social preference ordering becomes cyclical [$d \succ \mathrm{b} \succ c \succ a \succ d$]. So according to Kemeny's procedure *d* will be elected because according to Kemeny the most likely (transitive) social preference ordering is $d \succ b \succ c \succ a$ in which the sum (57) associated with the pairwise comparisons of this social preference ordering is highest. However, as the four absentee $d \succ b \succ c \succ a$ voters certainly prefer the election of *d*, their top–ranked candidate to the election of *a*, their lowest–ranked one, they are better off not voting —thereby demonstrating the vulnerability of Kemeny's procedure to the No–Show Paradox.

We also have here an instance of the Truncation Paradox. To show the vulnerability of Kemeny's procedure to this paradox suppose that the four voters with preference ordering $d \succ a \succ b \succ c$ list only their top preference (*d*). In this case one assumes that these voters are indifferent among *a*, *b*, and *c*, and as a result the social preference ordering becomes cyclical ($d \succ b \succ c \succ a \succ d$) and the most likely transitive social preference ordering will be topped by *d*, not by *a*, thereby demonstrating the vulnerability of Kemeny's procedure to the Truncation Paradox.

6.6.10 *Twin Paradox*

Example 6.6.10.1 shows the vulnerability of Kemeny's procedure to the Twin Paradox.

6.6.10.1 Example

Suppose there are 16 voters whose preference orderings among four candidates, *a*, *b*, *c*, *d*, are as follows:

No. of voters	Preference orderings
5	$d \succ b \succ c \succ a$
1	$d \succ a \succ b \succ c$
4	$b \succ c \succ a \succ d$
3	$a \succ d \succ c \succ b$
3	$a \succ d \succ b \succ c$

Here the social preference ordering is cyclical [$d \succ b \succ c \succ a \succ d$] and according to Kemeny's procedure the two most likely (transitive) social preference orderings are $d \succ b \succ c \succ a$ and $a \succ d \succ b \succ c$ because the sum (61) associated with the pairwise comparisons of these social preference orderings is highest. So according to Kemeny's procedure there is a tie between *a* and *d* (to be broken randomly).

Now suppose that, *ceteris paribus*, one twin brother of the $d \succ a \succ b \succ c$ voter joins the electorate, thereby, presumably, strengthening the position of d to be elected under Kemeny's procedure. But if this twin joins the electorate then a will be elected under Kemeny's procedure—thus demonstrating its vulnerability to the Twin Paradox. (*Ceteris paribus*, if one twin brother of the $d \succ a \succ b \succ c$ voter joins the electorate then the social preference ordering will still be cyclical but according to Kemeny's procedure the most likely transitive social preference ordering will be topped by a, not by d, thereby demonstrating the vulnerability of Kemeny's procedure to the Twin Paradox.)

6.6.11 SCC Paradox

Example 6.1.3.1 demonstrates the vulnerability of Kemeny's procedure to the SCC Paradox. In that example candidate d is elected according to Kemeny's procedure (because the "most likely" social preference ordering according to this procedure is $d \succ c \succ b \succ a$) but if, *ceteris paribus*, candidate b is eliminated then candidate a becomes the Absolute Majority Winner and is elected according to Kemeny's procedure—in violation of the SCC postulate.

6.7 The (In)Vulnerability of Schwartz's Procedure to Various Paradoxes

6.7.1 Condorcet Winner Paradox

The Condorcet Winner is clearly the smallest set of candidates not beaten by any candidate outside the set. Thus, the Condorcet Winner is always the Schwartz winner.

6.7.2 Absolute Majority Winner Paradox

Since the candidate ranked first by a majority of voters is the Condorcet Winner, the argument above applies.

6.7.3 Condorcet Loser Paradox

The Condorcet Loser cannot be an element of the set of Schwartz–winners since it is defeated by all other candidates. Hence, it cannot be a member of any top cycle.

6.7.4 *Absolute Majority Loser Paradoxes*

The Absolute Majority Loser is a special case of the Condorcet Loser and hence the above argument applies.

6.7.5 *Lack of Monotonicity Paradox*

"In case there is a Condorcet Winner, the procedure [Schwartz] chooses that alternative, and if the only admissible change in preferences moves that alternative up then it certainly remains the Condorcet Winner and will be chosen. If on the other hand, there is no Condorcet Winner to start with, and one of the alternatives in the Schwartz's choice set—say x—is moved higher in some individuals' preferences, *ceteris paribus*, then it cannot be the case that after the change some alternative which formerly did not beat x would now do so. Consequently, x still belongs to the Schwartz choice set, whereby monotonicity is satisfied" (Nurmi 1987, p. 72). This holds for fixed electorates. In variable electorates this procedure is vulnerable to monotonicity failure. For examples, see Felsenthal and Nurmi (2016, 2017).

6.7.6 *Preference Inversion Paradox*

Inverting all individual preferences inverts all pairwise comparison outcomes and hence the winners cannot be the same as in the original profile. Hence, the Preference Inversion Paradox is averted.

6.7.7 *Reinforcement Paradox*

Example 6.7.7.1 demonstrates the vulnerability of Schwartz's procedure to the Reinforcement Paradox.

6.7.7.1 Example

This example is due to Fishburn (1977, p. 483). Suppose there are two districts, I and II. In district I there are five voters, three of whom have preference orderings $x \succ y \succ w \succ z$ and the remaining two voters have preference orderings $z \succ y \succ w \succ x$. Since x constitutes here the top preference of an absolute majority of the voters, x will be elected in district I according to Schwartz's procedure.

In district II there are four voters: one with preference ordering $y \succ x \succ z \succ w$, one with preference ordering $w \succ y \succ x \succ z$, one with preference ordering $z \succ w \succ y \succ x$, and one with preference ordering $x \succ z \succ w \succ y$. The social preference ordering here is cyclical [$z \succ w \succ y \succ x \succ z$] so all four candidates should be in the choice set in district II according to Schwartz's procedure.

It would therefore be reasonable to assume that if, *ceteris paribus*, the two districts are amalgamated into a single district of nine voters, then x should be in the choice set of the amalgamated district according to Schwartz's procedure. However, in the amalgamated district y becomes the Condorcet Winner and hence is the only candidate in the choice set according to Schwartz's procedure—thus demonstrating its vulnerability to the Reinforcement Paradox.

6.7.8 No–Show and Twin Paradoxes

Example 6.7.8.1 demonstrates the vulnerability of Schwartz's procedure to the No–Show and Twin Paradoxes. Unlike the demonstration of these paradoxes under other procedures, in order to demonstrate the vulnerability of Schwartz's procedure to these paradoxes one must assume whether the voters are risk–neutral, risk–averse, or risk–seeking. We shall assume that the voters are risk–neutral, i.e., when only the voters' ordinal (but not cardinal) preferences are known, we assume that a voter whose ordinal preferences between three candidates, a, b, c is $a \succ b \succ c$ will be indifferent between obtaining a tie between these three candidates which will be broken randomly and the election of candidate b with certainty. Similarly, we assume that if this voter's ordinal preferences among four candidates is $b \succ c \succ d \succ a$ s/he would prefer the election of candidate c with certainty to obtaining a tie among all four candidates which will be broken randomly. Using different examples it is possible to demonstrate these paradoxes also when one assumes that the voters are risk–averse or risk–seeking.

6.7.8.1 Example

Suppose there are 100 voters whose preference orderings among four candidates, a, b, c, d, are as follows:

No. of voters	Preference orderings
23	$a \succ b \succ d \succ c$
28	$b \succ c \succ d \succ a$
49	$c \succ d \succ a \succ b$

Here the social preference ordering is cyclical [$a \succ b \succ c \succ d \succ a$] and according to Schwartz's procedure all four candidates belong to the choice set.

Now suppose that, *ceteris paribus*, four of the 28 $b \succ c \succ d \succ a$ voters decide not to participate in the election. In this case c becomes the Condorcet Winner—which the absentee voters certainly prefer over a tie among all candidates that will be broken randomly—thereby demonstrating the vulnerability of Schwartz's procedure to the No–Show Paradox.

We have here also a demonstration of the Twin Paradox. We just saw that, *ceteris paribus*, if there are only 24 voters with preference orderings $b \succ c \succ d \succ a$ then candidate c is the Condorcet Winner and is the only candidate belonging to the choice set according to Schwartz's procedure. But if, *ceteris paribus*, one adds another four clones with preference ordering $b \succ c \succ d \succ a$ then Schwartz's choice set includes all candidates—which is a less preferable outcome for these voters, thus demonstrating the vulnerability of Schwartz's procedure to the Twin Paradox.

6.7.9 Truncation and SCC Paradoxes

To demonstrate the vulnerability of Schwartz's procedure to the Truncation Paradox we use again Example 6.5.8.1. In the first part of this example we obtained that candidate d is the Condorcet Winner and hence is the sole candidate belonging to the Schwartz set. But, *ceteris paribus*, when two of the voters whose preference ordering is $e \succ b \succ a \succ d \succ c$ decide not to reveal their last two preferences (thereby assuming that the probability that they prefer d to c is equal to the probability they prefer c to d), one obtains the following expected paired comparisons matrix:

	a	b	c	d	e
a	–	10	9	6	0
b	6	–	9	6	0
c	7	7	–	8	4
d	10	10	8	–	10
e	16	16	12	6	–

As can be seen from this matrix only candidates d, e belong to the Schwartz set (because each of these candidates either beats or ties with each of the other three candidates)—which is a preferred outcome for the above–mentioned two truncating voters over the certain election of candidate d—thereby demonstrating the vulnerability of Schwartz's procedure to the Truncation Paradox.

This paired comparisons matrix can also be used to demonstrate the vulnerability of Schwartz's procedure to the SCC Paradox. We have just seen that according to this paired comparisons matrix only candidates d, e belong to the Schwartz set. However, if *ceteris paribus*, candidate c is eliminated (by deleting row c and column c from this matrix) then candidate d becomes the Condorcet Winner and is elected by Schwartz's procedure—in violation of the SCC postulate.

6.7.10 Pareto-Dominated Candidate Paradox

Example 6.7.10.1 demonstrates the vulnerability of Schwartz's procedure to the Pareto-Dominated Candidate Paradox.

6.7.10.1 Example

This example is due to Fishburn (1973, p. 89; 1977, p. 478). Suppose there are three voters whose preference orderings among four candidates, *a, b, c, d* are as follows:

No. of voters	Preference orderings
1	$a \succ b \succ c \succ d$
1	$d \succ a \succ b \succ c$
1	$c \succ d \succ a \succ b$

Here the social preference ordering is cyclical ($a \succ b \succ c \succ d \succ a$) and according to Schwartz's procedure all four candidates belong to the choice set—this despite the fact that candidate b is Pareto-dominated by a (because all voters prefer a to b)—thus demonstrating the vulnerability of this procedure to the Pareto-Dominated Candidate Paradox.

6.8 The (In)Vulnerability of Young's Procedure to Various Paradoxes

6.8.1 Condorcet Winner Paradox

Since the Condorcet Winner requires no removals of voters to become one, it is elected by Young's procedure.

6.8.2 Absolute Majority Paradox

The Absolute Majority Winner is a special case of Condorcet Winner and, hence, the above argument applies.

6.8.3 Pareto-Dominated Candidate Paradox

Suppose that x is Pareto-dominated by y. Then making x the Condorcet Winner will not succeed no matter how many voters are eliminated, while any alternative ranked first by at least one voter can be made the Condorcet Winner by eliminating at most v–1 voters. Hence x cannot be elected by Young's procedure.

6.8.4 Lack of Monotonicity Paradox

If x wins by Young's procedure and its position is improved, *ceteris paribus*, it remains the winner since the change in the profile does not affect the number of voters that need to be removed in order for other candidates to become Condorcet Winners. Candidate x, in contrast, may need fewer voters to be removed than at the outset. So, Young's method is monotonic in fixed electorates. In variable electorates Young's procedure, as a Condorcet extension, is vulnerable to monotonicity failures. For examples, see Felsenthal and Nurmi (2016, 2017).

6.8.5 Condorcet Loser, Absolute Loser and Preference Inversion Paradoxes

Example 6.1.2.1 can be used to demonstrate the vulnerability of Young's procedure to electing not only a Condorcet Loser but also an Absolute Majority Loser. In that example candidate d is an Absolute Majority Loser (and hence also a Condorcet Loser), but under Young's procedure d will be elected because for d to become a Condorcet Winner only two voters must be removed from the 11–voter electorate (any two voters whose last preference is d), whereas for each of the other three candidates more than two voters must be removed in order for them to become a Condorcet Winner.

Example 6.1.2.1 can also be used to demonstrate the vulnerability of Young's procedure to the Preference Inversion Paradox because, as we have already seen, if all voters in Example 6.1.2.1 invert their preference orderings then d becomes an Absolute Majority Winner and hence is elected under Young's procedure.

6.8.6 Reinforcement Paradox

Example 6.2.7.1 can be used, *mutatis mutandis*, to demonstrate the vulnerability of Young's procedure to the Reinforcement Paradox. In that example candidate x is a Condorcet Winner in district I and hence is elected in this district according to Young's procedure too. To become the Condorcet Winner in district II only five voters must be removed (any five voters who prefer y to x), whereas for any of the other candidates to become a Condorcet Winner in district II more than five voters must be removed. So according to Young's procedure candidate x is elected also in district II. But, as was demonstrated in Example 6.2.7.1, in the amalgamated district with 19 voters candidate *y* becomes the Condorcet Winner and is therefore elected also according to Young's procedure—thereby demonstrating its vulnerability to the Reinforcement Paradox.

6.8.7 *No–Show, Twin, Truncation, and SCC Paradoxes*

Example 6.8.7.1 demonstrates the vulnerability of Young's procedure to the No–Show, Twin, Truncation, and SCC Paradoxes.

6.8.7.1 Example

Suppose there are 39 voters whose preference orderings among five candidates, *a, b, c, d, e*, are as follows:

No. of voters	Preference orderings
11	$b \succ a \succ d \succ e \succ c$
10	$e \succ c \succ b \succ d \succ a$
10	$a \succ c \succ d \succ b \succ e$
2	$e \succ c \succ d \succ b \succ a$
2	$e \succ d \succ c \succ b \succ a$
2	$c \succ b \succ a \succ d \succ e$
1	$d \succ c \succ b \succ a \succ e$
1	$a \succ b \succ d \succ e \succ c$

These preference orderings can be depicted as the following paired comparisons matrix:

	a	*b*	*c*	*d*	*e*
a	–	11	22	24	25
b	28	–	12	24	25
c	17	27	–	24	13
d	15	15	15	–	25
e	14	14	26	14	–

The social preference ordering here is cyclical ($c \succ b \succ a \succ d \succ e \succ c$). The minimal number of voters one must remove in order for one of the five candidates to become a Condorcet Winner is 12 (the 10 voters whose top preference is *a* and the two voters whose top preference is *c*); these removals are needed in order for *e* to become the Condorcet Winner. So *e* is elected according to Young's procedure given this profile.

Now suppose that, *ceteris paribus*, 10 new voters whose preference orderings is $e \succ d \succ a \succ b \succ c$ join the electorate—thus presumably strengthening e's position. However, in this case we obtain the following paired comparisons matrix:

	a	b	c	d	e
a	–	21	32	24	25
b	28	–	22	24	25
c	17	27	–	24	13
d	25	25	25	–	25
e	24	24	36	24	–

which shows that candidate d is the Condorcet Winner, hence the 10 added voters are better off abstaining—thus demonstrating the vulnerability of Young's procedure to the No–Show Paradox.[4] Obviously twins are not always welcome here.

However, if the 10 added voters reveal only their top preference (e), then we obtain the following paired comparisons matrix:

	a	b	c	d	e
a	–	16	27	29	25
b	33	–	17	29	25
c	22	32	–	29	13
d	20	20	20	–	25
e	24	24	36	24	–

Here candidate e will be elected according to Young's procedure because for e to become the Condorcet Winner in this case only two voters must be removed (any two voters whose bottom preference is e), whereas for any of the other candidates to become a Condorcet Winner more than two voters must be removed—thus demonstrating that Young's procedure is vulnerable to the Truncation Paradox.

To demonstrate the vulnerability of Young's procedure to SCC let us look again at the paired comparison matrix of the 39 voters at the beginning of this example. We saw that given this matrix candidate e is elected under Young's procedure. Now suppose that, *ceteris paribus*, candidate b decides to withdraw from the race. But if, as a result, we cross out row b and column b in the paired comparison matrix, we see that candidate a becomes the Condorcet Winner and hence elected by Young's procedure—thereby demonstrating its vulnerability to SCC.

Table 6.1 summarizes the preceding discussion.

[4]The added 10 voters also demonstrate that Young's procedure violates what Pérez (1995, p. 143) has called the *Monotonicity property in face of new voters*. This property requires that if candidate x is chosen in a given situation and then, *ceteris paribus*, a new voter is added whose top preference is x, then: (1) x must remain chosen for *Weak Monotonicity* to be satisfied, and (2) x must remain chosen and no one not chosen before should be chosen now in order for *Monotonicity* to be satisfied.

Table 6.1 (In)Vulnerability of ranked condorcet-consistent voting procedures to 13 voting paradoxes

Paradox	Procedure							
	Minimax	Dodgson	Black	Copeland	Kemeny	Nanson	Schwartz	Young
Condorcet Winner Paradox	−	−	−	−	−	−	−	−
Absolute Majority Paradox	−	−	−	−	−	−	−	−
Condorcet Loser Paradox	⊕	⊕	−	−	−	−	−	⊕
Absolute Majority Loser Paradox	⊕	⊕	−	−	−	−	−	⊕
Pareto Dominated Candidate	−	−	−	−	−	−	⊕	−
Lack of Monotonicity	−	⊕	−	−	−	⊕	−	−
Reinforcement	+	+	+	+	+	+	+	+
No-Show	+	+	+	+	+	+	+	+
Twin	+	+	+	+	+	+	+	+
Truncation	+	+	+	+	+	+	+	+
SCC	+	+	+	+	+	+	+	+
Preference Inversion	+	+	−	−	−	−	−	+
Dependence on Order of Voting (DOV)	−	−	−	−	−	−	−	−
Total ⊕ signs	2	3	0	0	0	1	1	2
Total + & ⊕ signs	8	9	5	5	5	6	6	8

Notes

A + sign indicates that a procedure is vulnerable to the specified paradox;
A ⊕ sign indicates that a procedure is vulnerable to the specified paradox which seems to us an especially intolerable paradox;
A − sign indicates that a procedure is not vulnerable to the specified paradox;
It is assumed that all voters have linear preference ordering among all competing candidates.

Exercises

Problem 6.1 Construct a profile where the Plurality Voting procedure and Dodgson's rule result in different winners.

Problem 6.2 Consider the following 4–voter 5–alternative profile:

No. of voters	Preference orderings
2	$e \succ d \succ a \succ b \succ c$
1	$c \succ b \succ a \succ e \succ d$
1	$d \succ c \succ b \succ a \succ e$

(i) Which alternative will be chosen according to Copeland's procedure?
(ii) Assume now that, *ceteris paribus*, an additional voter with preference ordering $d \succ e \succ a \succ b \succ c$ joins the electorate. Would the previous winner be re–elected? If not, to which paradox would you say that Copeland's procedure is vulnerable?

Problem 6.3 Consider the following 14–voter 5–alternative profile:

No. of voters	Preference orderings
3	$d \succ e \succ a \succ b \succ c$
3	$e \succ a \succ c \succ b \succ d$
4	$c \succ d \succ e \succ a \succ b$
3	$d \succ e \succ b \succ c \succ a$
1	$e \succ b \succ a \succ d \succ c$

(i) Which alternative will be chosen according to Black's procedure?
(ii) Assume now that, *ceteris paribus*, two additional voters with preference ordering $e \succ b \succ a \succ d \succ c$ join the electorate. Would the previous winner be re-elected? If not, to which paradox would you say that Black's procedure is vulnerable?

Problem 6.4 Consider the following 15–voter 4–alternative profile:

No. of voters	Preference orderings
5	$d \succ b \succ c \succ a$
4	$b \succ c \succ a \succ d$
3	$a \succ d \succ c \succ b$
3	$a \succ d \succ b \succ c$

(i) Which alternative will be chosen according to Kemeny's procedure?
(ii) Assume now that, *ceteris paribus*, four additional voters with preference ordering $d \succ a \succ b \succ c$ join the electorate. Would the previous winner be re-elected? If not, to which paradox would you say that Kemeny's procedure is vulnerable?

Answers to Exercises

Problem 6.1 Here is an example:

No. of voters	Preference orderings
4	$a \succ b \succ c$
3	$b \succ c \succ a$
2	$c \succ b \succ a$

Here b is the Condorcet (and hence Dodgson) Winner, but a is the Plurality Voting winner.

Problem 6.2 This example is due to Felsenthal and Nurmi (2017, pp. 72–73). According to Copeland's procedure d is the winner (with 3 points). But as a result of the additional voter joining the electorate e becomes the Condorcet Winner and hence is elected according to Copeland's procedure—which demonstrates that this procedure is vulnerable to monotonicity failure in variable electorates.

Problem 6.3 This example is due to Felsenthal and Nurmi (2017, pp. 74–75). According to Black's procedure e is the winner (with 42 points). But as a result of the additional two voters joining the electorate d becomes the Condorcet Winner and hence is elected according to Black's procedure—which demonstrates that this procedure is vulnerable to monotonicity failure in variable electorates.

Problem 6.4 This example is due to Felsenthal and Nurmi (2017, pp. 76–77). According to Kemeny's procedure d is the winner (because the most likely social preference ordering is $d \succ b \succ c \succ a$). But as a result of the additional four voters joining the electorate a becomes the Condorcet Winner and hence is elected according to Kemeny's procedure—which demonstrates that this procedure is vulnerable to monotonicity failure in variable electorates.

References

Felsenthal, D. S. (2012). Review of paradoxes afflicting procedures for electing a single candidate. In D. S. Felsenthal & M. Machover (Eds.), *Electoral systems: Paradoxes, assumptions, and procedures*. Berlin Heidelberg: Springer, Ch. 3, pp. 19–92.

Felsenthal, D. S., & Nurmi, H. (2016). Two types of participation failure under nine voting methods in variable electorates. *Public Choice, 168*, 115–135.

Felsenthal, D. S., & Nurmi, H. (2017). *Monotonicity failures afflicting procedures for electing a single candidate*. Cham, Switzerland: Springer.

Fishburn, P. C. (1973). *The theory of social choice*. Princeton, N.J.: Princeton University Press.

Fishburn, P. C. (1974). Paradoxes of voting. *American Political Science Review, 68*, 537–546.

Fishburn, P. C. (1977). Condorcet social choice functions. *SIAM Journal on Applied Mathematics, 33*, 469–489.

Fishburn, P. C. (1982). Monotonicity paradoxes in the theory of elections. *Discrete Applied Mathematics, 4*, 119–134.

Nurmi, H. (1987). *Comparing voting systems*. Dordrect: D. Reidel.

Nurmi, H. (2012). On the relevance of theoretical results to voting system choice. In D. S. Felsenthal & M. Machover (Eds.), *Electoral systems: Paradoxes, assumptions, and procedures.* Berlin Heidelberg: Springer, Ch.10, pp. 255–274.

Pérez, J. (1995). Incidence of No–Show paradoxes in Condorcet choice functions. *Investigaciones Economicas, 19,* 139–154.

Saari, D. G., & Barney, S. (2003). Consequences of reversing preferences. *Mathematical Intelligencer, 25,* 17–31.

Smith, J. H. (1973). Aggregation of preferences with variable electorate. *Econometrica, 41,* 1027–1041.

Young, H. P., & Levenglick, A. (1978). A consistent extension of Condorcet's Election principle. *SIAM Journal of Applied Mathematics, 35,* 283–300.

Chapter 7
Summary

Abstract We discuss the findings of the preceding chapters aiming at an overall judgement of the relative merits of the 18 procedures in the light of their (in)vulnerability to various voting paradoxes. No procedure is invulnerable to all the analyzed voting paradoxes, but there are differences in the variety of paradoxes that various procedures are vulnerable to. It turns out that for those emphasizing that a Condorcet Winner ought to be elected when s/he exists, the most plausible voting procedures are associated with the names of Copeland and Kemeny, while for those stressing the need to preserve the basic rationale of voting, viz., the participation condition, the most appealing system is the Borda count.

Keywords Comparative evaluation of voting procedures · Voting paradoxes · (In)Vulnerability to voting paradoxes · Condorcet winner · Participation

As can be seen from Tables 4.1, 5.1 and 6.1, (cf. Chaps. 4, 5 and 6) eight procedures (Successive Elimination, Alternative Vote, Coombs, Bucklin, Majority Judgment, Minimax, Dodgson, and Young) are susceptible to the largest number of paradoxes (8–9), whereas five procedures (Plurality Voting (first–past–the–post), Borda, Black, Copeland, Kemeny) are susceptible to the smallest number of paradoxes (4–5).

Of the nine Condorcet–consistent procedures, six procedures (Successive Elimination, Minimax, Dodgson's, Nanson's, Schwartz's, and Young's) are dominated by the other three procedures (Black's, Copeland's and Kemeny's) in terms of the paradoxes to which these procedures are susceptible.

However, the number of paradoxes to which each of the various voting procedures surveyed here is vulnerable may be regarded as meaningless or even misleading. This is so for two reasons.

First, some paradoxes are but special cases of other paradoxes or may induce the occurrence of other paradoxes, as follows:

This chapter is partly based on Felsenthal (2012) and partly on Nurmi (2012).

D. S. Felsenthal and H. Nurmi, *Voting Procedures for Electing a Single Candidate*, SpringerBriefs in Economics, https://doi.org/10.1007/978-3-319-74033-1_7

- A procedure which is vulnerable to the Absolute Majority Winner Paradox is also vulnerable to the Condorcet Winner Paradox;
- A procedure which is vulnerable to the Absolute Majority Loser Paradox is also vulnerable to the Condorcet Loser Paradox;
- Except for the Range Voting and Majority Judgment procedures, all procedures surveyed in this book that are vulnerable to the Condorcet Loser Paradox are also vulnerable to the Preference Inversion Paradox.
- The five procedures surveyed in this book which may display lack of monotonicity are also susceptible to the No–Show Paradox[1];
- All Condorcet–consistent procedures are susceptible to the No–Show Paradox and hence also to the Twin Paradox when there exist at least four candidates.[2]

Second, and more importantly, not all the surveyed paradoxes are equally undesirable. Although assessing the severity of the various paradoxes is largely a subjective matter, *there seems to be a wide consensus that a voting procedure which is susceptible to an especially serious paradox (denoted by ⊕ in Tables* 4.1, 5.1, *and* 6.1 *in Chaps.* 4, 5 *and* 6*), i.e., a voting procedure which may elect a Pareto–dominated candidate, or elect a Condorcet (and Absolute) Loser, or display lack of monotonicity, or fail to elect an Absolute Majority Winner, should be disqualified as a reasonable voting procedure regardless of the probability that these paradoxes may occur.* On the other hand, the degree of severity that should be assigned to the remaining paradoxes should depend, *inter alia*, on the likelihood of their occurrence under the procedures that are vulnerable to them. Thus, for example, a procedure which may display a given paradox only when the social preference ordering is cyclical—as is the case for most of the paradoxes afflicting the Condorcet–consistent procedures—should be deemed more desirable (and the paradoxes it may display more tolerable) than a procedure which can display the same paradox when a Condorcet Winner exists.[3]

Sometimes a more "graded" approach to procedure evaluations have been suggested (Nurmi 2012, pp. 258–260; see also Lagerspetz 2004). The starting point in this approach is the binary comparison of two systems, say A and B, where the

[1]Campbell and Kelly (2002) devised a non–monotonic voting rule that does not exhibit the No–Show Paradox. However, as this method violates the anonymity and neutrality conditions and hence has not been considered seriously for actual use, we ignore it. The suggested method is bizarre in other respects as well, e.g. if all voters rank x last, it will be elected.

[2]Although all Condorcet–consistent procedures are also susceptible to the Reinforcement Paradox, there is no logical connection between this Paradox and the No–Show Paradox. As mentioned by Moulin (1988, pp. 54–55), when there are no more than three candidates there exist Condorcet–consistent procedures which are immune to both the No–Show and Twin Paradoxes, e.g., the Minimax procedure which elects the candidate to whom the smallest majority objects.

[3]However, in order to be able to state conclusively which of several voting procedures that are susceptible to the same paradox is more likely to display this paradox, one must know what are the necessary and/or sufficient conditions for this paradox to occur under the various compared procedures. Such knowledge is still lacking with respect to most voting procedures and paradoxes.

superiority of A with respect to B in terms of a criterion takes on degrees from the strongest to weakest as follows:

1. A satisfies the criterion, while B does not, that is, there are profiles where B violates the criterion, but under no profiles does A violate it.
2. In every profile where A violates the criterion, so does B, but not the other way around. This would mean that A dominates B in terms of the criterion at hand.
3. In practically all profiles where A violates the criterion, also B does, but not the other way around. One could say that A dominates B almost everywhere.
4. Under a plausible probability model (i.e., a hypothesis concerning the distribution of voter preferences), B violates the criterion with higher probability than A.
5. In those (political) cultures that can be expected to characterize the voting body we focus upon, B violates the criterion more frequently than A.

The items above focus on comparisons in terms of a single criterion. Reaching an overall judgment concerning all criteria presupposes a way of amalgamating the criterion–wise evaluations into an overall choice or ranking, that is, a multiple criterion decision method. In a way this brings us back to the general social choice problem.

Additional criteria which should be used in assessing the relative desirability of a voting procedure are what may be called *administrative–technical criteria*. The main criteria belonging to this category are the following:

Requirements from the voter: some voting procedures make it more difficult for the voter to participate in an election by requiring him/her to rank–order all competing candidates, whereas other procedures make it easier for the voter by requiring him/her to vote for just one candidate or for any candidate(s) s/he approves. In his early survey of voting systems, Nurmi (1983) introduced a similar "practical" criterion, viz., ballot easiness.

Ease of understanding how the winner is selected: In order to encourage voters to participate in an election a voting procedure must be transparent, i.e., voters must understand how their votes (preferences) are aggregated into a social choice. Thus a voting procedure where the winner is the candidate who received the plurality of votes is easier to explain—and is considered more transparent—than a procedure which may involve considerable mathematical calculations (e.g., Kemeny's) in order to determine the winner.

Ease of executing the elections: Election procedures requiring only one voting (or counting) round are more easily executed than election procedures that may require more than one voting (or counting) round. Similarly, election procedures requiring to count only the number of votes received by each candidate are easier to conduct than those requiring the conduct of all $n(n-1)/2$ paired contests between all n candidates, or those requiring the examination of up to $n!$ possible social preference orderings in order to determine the winner. Nurmi (1983) discusses briefly the computational complexity of determining the winner. Over the past couple of decades the computational complexity of social choice functions has been a major focus in the study of voting procedures (see e.g., Brandt et al. 2016).

Minimization of the temptation to vote insincerely: Although all voting procedures are vulnerable to manipulation, i.e., to the phenomenon where some voters may benefit if they vote insincerely, some voting procedures (e.g., Borda's count, Range

Voting) are susceptible to this considerably more than others. The incentives for preference misrepresentation depend, however, crucially on the accuracy and degree of detail of information concerning the preference distributions that the voters have at their disposal. For example, the Plurality Voting procedure requires very superficial information—only the distribution of first-ranked candidates—for successful misrepresentation, while the manipulation of Nanson's procedure can in general succeed only under nearly full information about the preference profile. Moreover, all misrepresentation efforts may backfire either by making no difference in the ensuing outcomes or by deteriorating the outcomes from the manipulators' point of view.

Discriminability: One should prefer a voting procedure which is more discriminate, i.e., it is more likely to select (deterministically) a unique winner than produce a set of tied candidates—in which case the employment of additional means are needed to obtain a unique winner. Thus, for example, when the social preference ordering is cyclical then, *ceteris paribus*, Schwartz's and Copeland's methods are considerably less discriminating than at least some of the remaining Condorcet–consistent procedures surveyed in this book.

Of course there may exist conflicts between some of these technical–administrative criteria. For example, a procedure like Kemeny's which, on the one hand, is more difficult to execute in practice and to explain to prospective voters (and hence less transparent), is, on the other hand, more discriminate and less vulnerable to insincere behavior.

So in view of all the above criteria, which of the 18 surveyed voting procedures do we think should be preferred? Since the weakest extension of the majority rule principle when there are more than two candidates is the Condorcet Winner principle, many scholars think that the electoral system which ought to be used for electing one out of $n \geq 2$ candidates should be Condorcet–consistent. Others are not convinced, some basing their judgement on Fishburn's (1973) finding that sometimes Condorcet Winners may be positionally dominated by other alternatives and on Saari's analyses pointing to the bizarre variation of Condorcet Winners when Condorcet components are added to or subtracted from a profile with a (possibly even strong) Condorcet Winner (cf. Saari 1995; 2008, pp. 155–160). In fact, according to Saari all procedures based on binary comparisons lose information about a crucial aspect of voter opinions: their transitivity. Indeed, since pairwise comparisons are unable to discriminate alternative pairs extracted from complete and transitive rankings from those that are cyclic, all positional information is set aside in determining the winners of pairwise procedures: e.g., if an individual has an intransitive preference relation $a \succ b \succ c \succ a$ the pairwise comparison procedures do not distinguish this from the transitive ranking $a \succ b \succ c$. When determining the winner by conducting a pairwise comparison, say, between a and b, the procedures ignore the information not only about how many candidates are between a and b in individual preferences or about whether they both are at the high or low end of the orderings, but—most importantly—about whether the votes in favor of each candidate stem from transitive or intransitive relations. This positional information is more fully utilized in positional procedures, especially in the Borda count. Thus, as stated earlier, the normative principle underlying the Borda count (and similar positional systems) is that the winner ought to be that candidate who occupies the highest position, *on average*, in the rankings of the voters.

Fishburn's (1973, p. 147) example showing that the Condorcet Winner is not necessarily the most plausible choice involves five voters and five candidates in the following profile:

1 voter: $d \succ e \succ a \succ b \succ c$
1 voter: $e \succ a \succ c \succ b \succ d$
1 voter: $c \succ d \succ e \succ a \succ b$
1 voter: $d \succ e \succ b \succ c \succ a$
1 voter: $e \succ b \succ a \succ d \succ c$

Here d is the Condorcet Winner and yet the Borda Winner, e, has as many first ranks (2) as d, more second and third ranks than d and no lower than third ranks. So, arguably the choice of e (whose average ranking is 1.8) instead of d (whose average ranking is 2.6) would be quite plausible.[4]

Suppose that one adheres to the former contention that a Condorcet Winner should always be elected if one exists. But as one does not know before an election is conducted whether a Condorcet Winner will exist or whether the social preference ordering will contain a top cycle, which of the nine Condorcet–consistent procedures surveyed and exemplified in this book should be preferred in case a top cycle exists? In this case we think that the Successive Elimination procedure and Schwartz's procedure should be readily disqualified because of their vulnerability to electing a Pareto–dominated candidate, Dodgson's and Nanson's procedures should be readily disqualified because of their lack of monotonicity, and the Minimax, Dodgson's and Young's procedures should be readily disqualified because of their vulnerability to electing a Condorcet Loser or even an Absolute Loser. Although Black's procedure cannot elect a Condorcet Loser, it may nevertheless come quite close to it because, as demonstrated in Example 6.5.11.1 (Chap. 6), it violates Smith's (1973) Condorcet principle, so this procedure too seems to us considerably more desirable than the Minimax, Dodgson's and Young's procedures. It should be observed, though, that benefiting from preference misrepresentation is in general very difficult under Dodgson's and Nanson's procedures. Surely, this is an advantage that should be reckoned with. Moreover, Pérez (2001) singles out the Minimax and Young's procedures as less vulnerable to extreme forms of No–Show Paradoxes and Felsenthal and Nurmi (2017) have shown that this applies to Dodgson's and Nanson's procedures as well.

[4]When there are n candidates each of whom can be ranked by each of the v voters as either 1, 2, …, n, then the maximal *average rank* a candidate can obtain under Borda's procedure is 1 (if all voters rank the same candidate at the top of their preference ordering) and the lowest *average rank* a candidate can obtain is n (if all voters rank the same candidate at the bottom of their preference ordering). It is of course possible that the Condorcet Winner and the Borda winner will have the same average rank.

This leaves those emphasizing the importance of the Condorcet Winner criterion with a choice between the remaining two Condorcet–consistent procedures—Copeland's and Kemeny's. The choice between them depends on the importance one assigns to the above–mentioned technical–administrative criteria. Both these procedures require voters to rank–order all candidates. However, Copeland's method is probably easier than Kemeny's to explain to lay voters, as well as, when the number of candidates is large, may involve considerably fewer calculations in determining who is (are) the ultimate winner(s). Kemeny's procedure, on the other hand, is more discriminate than Copeland's when the number of candidates is relatively small, and is probably also—because of its increased complexity in determining the ultimate winner—less vulnerable to insincere voting. So if we would have to choose between these two procedures we would choose Kemeny's because most elections where a single candidate must be elected usually involve relatively few contestants—in which case Kemeny's procedure seems to have an advantage over Copeland's procedure. Moreover, as mentioned in the description of Kemeny's procedure and as argued by Young (1995, pp. 60–62), Kemeny's procedure has also the advantage that it can be justified not only from Condorcet's perspective of the maximum likelihood rule, but also as choosing for the entire society the "median preference ordering"—which can be viewed from the perspective of modern statistics as the best compromise between the various rankings reported by the voters. So, for those emphasizing Condorcet's winning concept, this train of thought would seem to lead to advocating Kemeny's procedure. This conclusion should, however, be tempered with the observation that, as all Condorcet extensions, Kemeny's procedure is vulnerable to nearly all forms of No–Show Paradoxes. So, it might be a challenge to recommend to a layman to adopt a system which is (demonstrably) very difficult to apply and by which the voter might even be better off by not voting at all than by revealing his/her preferences.

For those not regarding the Condorcet–consistency an essential desirable property of voting systems, the Borda count seems clearly superior to other positional systems. Its main flaw among those criteria we have employed is the vulnerability to the Absolute Majority Winner Paradox. However, according to Saari (1995) this is not an essential flaw. Absolute Majority Winners may be disposed of and replaced by new Condorcet Winners by adding to or removing from profiles sub–profiles that constitute a perfectly symmetric Condorcet Paradox and yet, intuitively, such profiles constitute a perfect tie among the candidates (see Saari 1995; for a simplified exposition of some of the arguments in Saari's *Geometry of Voting* book, see Nurmi 1999, 31–40).

To see this, consider the following example involving an Absolute Majority Winner.

5 voters: $a \succ b \succ c$
3 voters: $b \succ c \succ a$

Obviously a is the Absolute Majority Winner, while b is the Borda winner. Introduce now a group of nine voters whose preferences constitute a perfectly symmetrical Condorcet Paradox (cyclical) profile:

3 voters: $a \succ c \succ b$
3 voters: $b \succ a \succ c$
3 voters: $c \succ b \succ a$

Because of the symmetry we have no reason to rank any candidate ahead of any other in the latter profile since each candidate is ranked equally many (3) times first, second and third. So, on the basis of the available information we have to conclude that the latter profile is a 3–way tie.

Now add the latter profile to the former to obtain a 17–voter voting body with the following profile:

5 voters: $a \succ b \succ c$
3 voters: a $\succ c \succ b$
3 voters: $b \succ a \succ c$
3 voters: $b \succ c \succ a$
3 voters: $c \succ b \succ a$

We observe that there is a Condorcet Winner in the amalgamated profile, viz., *b*. Thus, adding a perfectly tied profile to one with an Absolute Majority Winner makes the latter a non–winner under any Condorcet extension procedure. At the same time the Borda winner, *b*, remains a robust winner under this kind of profile modification.

So, Condorcet Winners—even strong ones, i.e., an Absolute Majority Winner—can be "destroyed" by adding to, or subtracting from, a given profile with such a winner a sub–profile that constitutes a perfectly symmetric Condorcet Paradox. Given that the Borda winners are not similarly sensitive to such profile modifications, one may well regard the Borda count as a plausible social choice method.

However, the Borda count is readily subject to manipulation given sufficiently detailed information about the preference profile. To see this consider the simple example where three voters have (sincere) preference order $a \succ b \succ c$ and two voters have (sincere) preference order $b \succ c \succ a$—and that all voters are aware of each other's preference ordering. In this case the three $a \succ b \succ c$ voters know that under Borda's procedure *b* will be elected if all voters rank the candidates sincerely, so to avoid *b*'s election they will be tempted to misrepresent their preference orderings to $a \succ c \succ b$ thereby ensuring that their top alternative (*a*) will be elected. In general, voters can gain under the Borda count by ranking the most serious rival of their favorite candidate last in order to lower his or her point total (Black 1958; Ludwin 1978; Brams and Fishburn 1991). This strategy is relatively easy to execute, unlike a manipulative strategy under some of the other ranked voting procedures we analyzed (e.g., Alternative Vote, Coombs, Nanson) which require estimating who is likely to be eliminated, and in what order, so as to be able to exploit these procedures' dependence on sequential eliminations. Black (1958, pp. 237–238) reports that "When some members of the Academy suggested to Borda that his scheme was satisfactory in theory but would not work in practice because people would misrepresent their true valuations in their voting so as to help their own candidate, he has replied 'My scheme is intended only for honest men'." (cf. also Black 1958, p. 182).

Another type of paradox, not mentioned previously, that afflicts the Borda count and related point–assignment systems involves manipulability by changing the agenda. For example, the introduction of a new candidate, who cannot win—and, consequently, would appear irrelevant—can completely reverse the point–total order of the old candidates, even though there are no changes in the voters' rankings of these candidates. To see this, consider the following example (adapted from Fishburn 1974, p. 540):

Suppose there are seven voters whose preference orderings among three candidates are as follows:

No. of voters	Preference orderings
2	$a \succ c \succ b$
2	$b \succ a \succ c$
3	$c \succ b \succ a$

Here the Borda winner is c (with 8 points). Now suppose that an "irrelevant" candidate, x, is introduced, thus:

No. of voters	Preference orderings
2	$a \succ x \succ c \succ b$
2	$b \succ a \succ x \succ c$
3	$c \succ b \succ a \succ x$

As a result of introducing x the Borda winner becomes a (with 13 points), so it is clearly in the interest of a's supporters to encourage x to enter simply to ensure a's victory.

In sum, for those scholars and practitioners who give primary importance to guaranteeing that eventual Condorcet Winners be always elected, it seems to us that of the 18 (deterministic) voting procedures analyzed in this book, the Condorcet–consistent procedures proposed by Copeland (1951) and by Kemeny (1959) are undoubtedly the most desirable from a social–choice perspective for electing one out of several candidates. For those concerned about the Participation principle—and hence about the fundamental motivation to vote, the positional procedures, especially the Borda count, seem to us more appealing.

Exercises

Problem 7.1 Are trivial or dictatorial voting procedures manipulable?

Problem 7.2 Show that the Plurality with Runoff procedure is manipulable.

Problem 7.3 Show that there are profiles where the agenda–controller can bring about any outcome when the Successive Elimination procedure is used under the assumption that the voters are sincere.

Answers to Exercises

Problem 7.1 Trivial procedures result in a fixed outcome regardless of preferences. Misrepresenting one's preference cannot, therefore, improve the outcome. Dictatorial procedures always result in the outcome most preferred by the dictator. Hence, no non–dictatorial voter can improve upon the outcome that the dictator determines. The dictator, on the other hand, has no incentive to misrepresent his/her preference.

Problem 7.2 Consider the following profile:

No. of voters	Preference orderings
2	$a \succ b \succ c$
1	$b \succ a \succ c$
2	$c \succ b \succ a$

With sincere voting a wins. With one voter of the last group voting as if his/her preference is $b \succ a \succ c$, *ceteris paribus*, the outcome is b, i.e. better than a for this voter.

Problem 7.3 The Condorcet Paradox profile is perhaps the simplest example:

No. of voters	Preference ordering
1	$a \succ b \succ c$
1	$b \succ c \succ a$
1	$c \succ a \succ b$

If the agenda–controller wants a to win, he/she sets the agenda: (i) b versus c, (ii) the winner of (i) versus a. If he/she wants b to win, he/she sets the agenda: (i) a versus c, (ii) the winner of (i) versus b. If he/she wants c to win, his/her agenda is: (i) a versus b, (ii) the winner of (i) versus c.

References

Black, D. (1958). *The theory of committees and elections*. Cambridge: Cambridge University Press.

Brams, S. J., & Fishburn, P. C. (1991). Alternative voting systems. In L. Sandy Maisel (Ed.), *Political parties and elections in the United States: An encyclopedia*, vol. 1. New York: Garland, pp. 23–31.

Brandt, F., Conitzer, V., Endriss, U., Lang, J., & Procaccia, A. D. (Eds.). (2016). *Handbook of computational social choice*. New York: Cambridge University Press.

Campbell, D. E., & Kelly, J. S. (2002). Non–monotonicity does not imply the No–Show paradox. *Social Choice and Welfare, 19*, 513–515.

Copeland, A. H. (1951). A 'reasonable' social welfare function, *mimeographed*. University of Michigan, Department of Mathematics, Seminar on Applications of Mathematics to the Social Sciences.
Felsenthal, D. S. (2012). Review of paradoxes afflicting procedures for electing a single candidate. In D. S. Felsenthal & M. Machover (Eds.), *Electoral systems: Paradoxes, assumptions, and procedures*. Berlin Heidelberg: Springer, Ch. 3, pp. 19–92.
Felsenthal, D. S., & Nurmi, H. (2017). *Monotonicity failures afflicting procedures for electing a single candidate*. Cham, Switzerland: Springer.
Fishburn, P. C. (1973). *The theory of social choice*. Princeton, N.J.: Princeton University Press.
Fishburn, P. C. (1974). Paradoxes of voting. *American Political Science Review, 68*, 537–546.
Kemeny, J. G. (1959). Mathematics without numbers. *Daedalus, 88*, 577–591.
Lagerspetz, E. (2004). Evaluating voting systems. In M. Wiberg (Ed.), *Reasoned choices* (pp. 201–222). Helsinki: The Finnish Political Science Association.
Ludwin, W. G. (1978). Strategic voting and the Borda method. *Public Choice, 33*, 85–90.
Moulin, H. (1988). Condorcet's principle implies the No–Show paradox. *Journal of Economic Theory, 45*, 53–64.
Nurmi, H. (1983). Voting procedures: A summary analysis. *British Journal of Political Science, 13*(2), 181–208.
Nurmi, H. (1999). *Voting paradoxes and how to deal with them*. Berlin, Heidelberg, New York: Springer Verlag.
Nurmi, H. (2012). On the relevance of theoretical results to voting system choice. In D. S. Felsenthal & M. Machover (Eds.), *Electoral systems: Paradoxes, assumptions, and procedures*. Berlin Heidelberg: Springer, Ch. 10, pp. 255–274.
Pérez, J. (2001). The strong no show paradoxes are common flaw in Condorcet voting correspondences. *Social Choice and Welfare, 18*, 601–616.
Saari, D. G. (1995). *Basic Geometry of Voting*. New York: Springer Verlag.
Saari, D. G. (2008). *Disposing dictators, demystifying voting paradoxes: Social choice analysis*. New York: Cambridge University Press.
Smith, J. H. (1973). Aggregation of preferences with variable electorate. *Econometrica, 41*, 1027–1041.
Young, H. P. (1995). Optimal voting rules. *Journal of Economic Perspectives, 9*(1), 51–63.

The manufacturer's authorised representative in the EU is Springer Nature Customer Service Centre GmbH, Europaplatz 3, 69115 Heidelberg, Germany. If you have any concerns regarding our products, please contact ProductSafety@springernature.com

Printed and bound by CPI Group (UK) Ltd, Croydon, CR0 4YY
30/09/2026
02225606-0015